THE DETECTIVE IN THE DOORYARD

Reflections of a Maine Cop

Timothy Cotton

Down East Books

Camden, Maine

Down East Books

Published by Down East Books
An imprint of Globe Pequot
Trade division of The Rowman & Littlefield Publishing Group, Inc.
4501 Forbes Blvd., Ste. 200
Lanham, MD 20706
www.rowman.com
www.downeastbooks.com

Distributed by NATIONAL BOOK NETWORK

ISBN 978-1-60893-742-4 (hardcover)
ISBN 978-1-60893-743-1 (e-book)

♾™ The paper used in this publication meets the minimum requirements of American National Standard for Information Sciences—Permanence of Paper for Printed Library Materials, ANSI/NISO Z39.48-1992.

Printed in the United States of America.

This book is dedicated to anyone who was
ever picked last—for anything—
and refused to let that day define them.

Contents

How It Came To Be—An Introduction

A theme you might notice as you thumb through my book of this and that is that much of what I write is borne from thoughts that come and go as I drive or ride, covering the miles between all the places I love to go.

None of these places are particularly exciting; they are just the places I love to go. I enjoy driving, the farther the better.

It's a couple of hours to my camp if I go through Ellsworth. It's a longer distance, but a shorter ride, if I go down Route 9. This is due to the higher speed limits. There are many variations of the trip available to me. All of them will inevitably get me "Down East" sooner or later.

I generally prefer later. I stopped rushing in my forties.

You can certainly talk about miles to a destination when in Maine, but it's not an accurate measurement of most trips. Here, we speak of time and distance as if they were one entity.

For example:

You: "How far is it to your brother-in-law's cabin?"

Me: "About an hour and a half or so. It depends on whether we stop in Harrington. It's not a bad ride. The cheapest gas is at the place on the corner of Route 1 and Route 182. They have pretty good coffee, so it makes sense to stretch out a bit there. I know the night clerk; he used to be a cop."

You: "Good talk. Gotta run."

I find that my favorite written phrases are forced out of the gravel-strewn corners of my brain by the early-evening cross breezes force-fed at fifty-five miles per hour through properly vented side windows. The words collect in a low spot, and I try to sweep them up into story piles before they are strewn around again by the subtle bumps of passing time. Many have been lost because I did not write them down in a timely manner.

Hours spent behind the wheel gives me much time for reflection. Words become more pliable as the sun strikes them at the proper angle as it streams through a grubby and sand-dimpled windshield. Songs that show up on the radio, like surprise guests at a family gathering, are fertilizer for the sentences that constantly expand and contract in my mind.

I have learned not to chase lost stories and fleeting thoughts. If I drive long enough, some of them come back to me. There are times when I feel a shiver up my spine as a story returns, like seeing an old dog return after it was believed to be lost. It is a joyous occasion.

Those are the nights I lose track of time, writing at a frantic pace in my effort to collect and store them in the hard drive before they run off again—heading off to the late-night convenience store for chips and Diet Coke. Some never return.

It is also possible that those fleeting stories were never mine to write. Maybe they were just passing through, like me, and headed off into the distance in search of someone else to document them. I can only hope that they were collected and incarcerated on paper before being lost at sea somewhere near Greenland.

For a long time in my life, I allowed my fear of screwing up sentences to stymie my desire to recollect, reflect, and document my thoughts, and memories. I always wrote police reports in vivid detail, leaning toward directly quoting victims, witnesses, and suspects. Not only did it save me from trying to say the same thing twice, but it also allowed those folks to be heard exactly as they had spoken.

The daily writing became more necessary when I found myself in charge of the Bangor Police Department Facebook page in the spring of 2014. I changed the way we presented a police department page. Along the way we collected more than 300,000 followers. Many came for the Duck of Justice. I'll write more about that later. I would be remiss if I did not explain the dynasty that the Duck has become.

Some people came, and stayed, for the odd bit of writing, which I determined would be a test of what fans would accept. I have been humbled by the response. You see, I am not a writer. I always refer to myself as a cop who writes stuff. I decided to tell our story by sharing and reflecting on the stories of the folks who interact with us, sometimes in a positive manner.

Let's be upfront about the early stages of this Facebook thing: grammarians and aficionados of proper comma usage came at me relentlessly. Don't get me wrong, many times they were correct. But I write the way I write, and with so many others who were stopping by to read the rambling, disconnected thoughts, I was able to power through and continue to present my ideas through the art of placing the written word on the interweb.

Some people even liked it.

This led to many accolades for our agency as we were trying something new and different. Now, many, many police departments have changed the way they present their profiles through social media. Some have taken it to new levels with high-quality productions made with expensive video and editing equipment. Some of them are hilarious.

I chose not to go that route, and was determined to stick with a writing-centric approach because it worked for us. I suspect as time goes on, and the next sucker takes over the page, my writing will be relegated to the Rubbermaid trash can in the kitchen of the police department. It's big enough to hold much of what I have done, and it's inevitable that things will change.

I can accept that.

I have had my fill of writing for immediate gratification. I get up early to write at least something on most days. Long before people go to work, I am contemplating some new way to share a message, a story, or a humorous tidbit. At some point, my mind agrees with my fingers, and we type directly into the Facebook machine. The lack of editing shows. I think it shows that I am like most folks, mainly because I *am* like most folks: flawed, thoughtful at times, and generally a nuisance to people who have White-Out correction fluid coursing through their veins.

Had I not become the public information officer and been assigned to write the Facebook updates, my less-than-stellar career as a student could have been forgotten. It should be.

I was a lackluster learner, especially when instructed to try to do better in my use of proper grammar and syntax.

I was an adamant minimalist during my formative years. I believe I was well-liked, even while being ejected from classes too many times to count, usually for cutting up, speaking out of turn, and generally being disruptive—oh, and forgetting where I left my homework. I never once laid blame on the dog.

I know my writing is destined to be slashed to bits by someone who actually paid attention in grammar and composition courses. I have laughed, far more than many times, that I ended up writing anything that was being presented on such a large forum and making it through a day without being deleted by the folks who know better.

The only thing that has saved me from doom is that I was a voracious reader. My grandmother Leora noticed this. She signed me up for a *Reader's Digest* subscription when I was nine years old. She had seen me poring through the stacks of books and periodicals at my grandparents' home. She also began to cut out all of Erma Bombeck's columns from the Lewiston *Sun Journal* and took the time to send them to me, tucked away in perfectly presented cursive-filled letters to her daughter, my mother.

Back in 2016, after I wrote something that struck a chord on a more national level, I was selected as the Humor Writer of the Month by the University of Dayton's Erma Bombeck Writer's Workshop. It was touching—and possibly made me tear up a little bit—when I thought of my grandmother's thin hands using shears (we call them scissors, Leora called them shears) to clip out humorous tidbits for her grandson, who was living a couple hundred miles away in Machias, Maine.

I am not, in any way, comparing my writing to that of Bombeck, but sarcastic humor, presented kindly, is often more willingly accepted by the masses than the angry, curse-filled diatribes that can be humorous, yet also hurtful.

Leora probably saw the notification of my selection from her vantage-point in the retired Salvation Army officer quarters of her celestial second home. She said something like, "Oh, my stars, Coleman, look at this! That little skinamalink must have read at least some of those clippings."

And I had. I read them all.

I suspect I was one of a very few elementary school students who had a collection of newspaper columns tucked away in his stack of *Reader's Digests* near the head of his unmade bed. But I was also a BB-gun-toting neighborhood menace. My grandmother was never pleased with my dark side.

I always loved to write essays. In true Cotton fashion, I was late turning in many (most) assignments. My goal was as simple as I was; I wanted to get just enough done to successfully complete each course. When looked at from that vantage point, I was a stellar performer: meeting goals, making friends, and having some laughs. I wish now that I had worked harder at all of it—well, not the laughs; I think I wrung out all of those I could, even when it was a bad idea.

A good editor will knock the living daylights out of most of my run-on sentences. You can probably see why it took me so long to find someone who would seriously consider collecting some of my writings and putting them into book form.

On the way to wherever we are now, I spoke to some pleasant people who work in the publishing industry. They called me, somewhat confused and less-than-intrigued about the Maine cop who writes poorly constructed but sometimes popular missives. I sensed their alarm when they spoke to me, soon realizing that I was probably not what they were looking for in a future bestseller.

I am comfortable telling people the truth about what they are getting themselves into.

I stated pretty much the same thing to each of them. Anyone can write a book; I want mine to sell. I was not comfortable that it would. In the meantime, I decided to continue writing on Facebook. It has been a delightful experience.

Some that I spoke to wanted me to write other things: fiction, novellas, how-to tips, a children's series, etc. When dealing with the individuals who seemed seriously interested in helping me get published, I listened. But I was fully aware which essays I had written seemed to strike a chord with the folks who showed up every single day to read the things shared by a Maine cop.

I have started a couple of fiction projects. I am beginning to really enjoy those stories, and I hope someday someone will come along who wants to publish one, or twelve, of them.

You are reading this, printed on paper, today because I chose to work with a Maine publishing house and an editor who called me because he saw a collection of new and old essays, snippets from "Got Warrants?," and some of my cop-related short stories as the basis for a marginally successful book.

I hope you can find some time to read all of it. Reach out to let me know whether you liked it or not. Some of my run-ons have been allowed to stay. I say that it's part of the charm, but you know that it's because I never cared for the diagraming of sentences. I am much more interested in collecting the thoughts and the stories before they slip away.

I know in my heart that the essays and stories that dwell between the covers of this book were destined to be mine to write.

Prelude to the Duck of Justice

Maybe you picked this book up on a whim. I tend to do the same thing when it comes to reading material. I don't review the *New York Times* bestseller list. If you were to peruse the list to find something that I had previously written, there would be much disappointment for you to overcome.

I've already worked through it, at least emotionally.

However, if you intended to pick this up, you already know that most of what I have written—to the delight of several people, not even counting my mom—has come to you via the Bangor Police Department Facebook page. Somewhere along the way, when a few folks were foolish enough to ask me to write intermittent blog-posts for a couple of cool websites, I wrote and enjoyed it immensely. The question is: How did we get here from there?

Some people think it was meant to be, but I firmly believe that this strange little journey, culminating in this bound collection, happened completely by mistake. I am not sold on social media, and I did not take over the department page because anyone expected magnificent results. I took over the page because it was included in my job assignment when I was promoted to sergeant after spending twelve years in the Criminal Investigation Division. If there were a period of time in my career, outside of the first few years as a young patrol officer, that I loved, it was during my time as a detective.

I waited until I was in my early fifties to make an attempt at being promoted from a simple, semi-sanguine, and sometimes sarcastic investigator to the rank of sergeant. Even during the process, I was less than excited to remove myself from what I enjoyed the most about being a cop.

While others in my age group were delightfully working their way through the ranks, I was just pleased to be an investigator. I became accustomed to being questioned by friends and family about why I had not yet become a sergeant. My answers varied, depending on whether or not they cared—most didn't—about my career advancement. Looking in from the outside of any career field, people assume that true success requires moving into management. I felt completely at home just working the cases.

I believe loving your job, no matter what it is, is far more satisfying than moving up. I don't think that happiness is hinged on an impressive title.

I had a pretty good success rate at getting confessions from suspects who did bad things to other people, and my job satisfaction was at its highest level when I could close a case quickly by using the art of pleasant conversation with not-so-pleasant people.

While crime scene investigation programs have become the rage on television, I was, and still am, a firm believer that people will tell you the truth about what they did if you take some time, build rapport, and allow them to tell you as many stories as they want to. I never use the term "interrogate," because I rarely did that. It makes for wonderful drama during primetime, but it is very unusual for people to spill the beans to someone they don't like. I tried to remain likable to even the most heinous of characters. It worked well.

A point I reiterate to newly minted detectives is that they need to go into a room with a suspect with the intention of finding something to actually like about that person. Movies and television paint a grim picture of the relationship between police and suspects. If you believe that there needs to be animosity between the opposing voices of a cop and a suspect, you will have a difficult time getting to the truth of any matter. If you can find a common thread and allow it to be woven into the sometimes-contentious conversation, it will be far easier for someone to tell you the truth.

After all, it is the truth we seek, nothing more.

I have included some stories in this book that will highlight the bond that can form between a cop and a suspect. It does not minimize the crime or change the fact that they must be held accountable for their misdeeds. It is merely a means to an end, a tool of the trade.

If there were a television program that showed the true art of simple conversation leading to a confession, it would be the 1970s series, *Columbo*. Peter Falk always portrayed himself as a dimwit with the suspects he interacted with. The lieutenant's shtick was that he was always kind and polite. He built rapport by talking about subjects that had nothing at all to do with the incident at hand.

If you offered me the choice between participating in a late-night raid into the den of criminality, or speaking to the arrestees for hours on end, I would always choose the latter. Through the years, I turned many a pleasant conversation into a confession, later to become a conviction.

The reason I changed my direction was that I felt it was time to move along from the detective division, and, while I ended up back there as the lieutenant in charge in 2017, it has never been the same. It was my realization of the inevitable changing of the guard all around me that made me take the sergeant's examination in 2014. I was selected from a list of great candidates to fill that role at the Bangor Police Department. I have to say it's been an honor and privilege to do so.

There was only one sergeant's position open when I was offered the promotion. The job was that of the public information officer. I was no stranger to talking for a living, since I had spent my formative years as a radio announcer. I also did a stint as an assistant news director at Stephen King's rock and roll radio station, where I also made a fool of myself on an '80s morning radio show with my good friend, Bobby Russell. We were pretty successful in our time slot, and Bobby is still doing the morning show in Bangor. Together we had some incredible times in the waning years of AM radio.

If you think that I learned the art of effective communication in a college program for cops, you will be disappointed in my story.

I attribute my success as a conversationalist to the many years of paying no attention in school and to my years in the studio while working in broadcasting. Spending four to six hours a day talking into a microphone to thousands of listeners is a pretty good way to become skilled at filling in the quiet spots during conversations with people who really don't want to share intimate details of their crimes. If things become really tense, I could talk about the murderer's favorite song from high school. Having a working knowledge of the hits, from all genres, has helped me build rapport with many people.

No one ever called me the Casey Kasem for Killers, but it has a nice ring to it.

Since I was no stranger to dealing with local media, and I could write a reasonable sentence (though I do have my detractors), I accepted the job that no one else wanted.

I was then told that I was going to be responsible for updating the Facebook page.

I had no experience with social media—I was a fifty-something has-been detective. The folks who had previously run our page did an admirable job with keeping it current. We had about 9,000 folks following us, which was nothing to sneeze at in a city with a population of 33,000.

I looked to other police pages for clues on how to make our presence on the interweb relevant and appealing. I found no good answers.

The chief, who has let me run free with my ideas, told me that I should avoid all topics that have anything to do with religion or politics. That seemed reasonable to me. There were no other directions given.

I determined, after much staring in disbelief at the emptiness of our page, that I would try to tell stories. I wanted to tell our story, but, more importantly, I wanted to tell the stories of the people we encountered on a daily basis.

I decided to use the same skills I had used to build rapport with suspects over the years. To do this, I used far too many words, very few photographs, and I attempted to employ the sarcastic, yet gentle, humor that I thought might make someone sit up and take notice.

They did notice. We were thrust into a strange and sudden limelight with people who found my verbosity, excessive comma usage, and strangely constructed sentences to be exactly what they were looking for.

Enter, stage right, a thirty-year-old stuffed American wood duck. Things were about to get a little strange on the now-marginally famous Bangor Police Department Facebook page.

The Duck of Justice

To understand how a taxidermied duck—as dead and stuffed as it is—became the renowned representative of the Bangor Police Department, you would have to travel back in time. In the late 1980s, I made the decision to become a police officer. The reasons were varied, and none too exciting. Working in radio had been a reasonable way to make a living, and I admit that I miss that period of my life. Once I extricated myself from radio and became a full-time police officer, I was a regular visitor to the Penobscot County District Attorney's office.

All criminal cases in those days, even traffic tickets, had to go through the DA's office for review. Cases could be sent back to an officer for more information, some would be filed with the courts after the criminal complaint was approved and written, and there were always subpoenas being served and returned by all of the area law enforcement agencies.

Kristine (last name withheld because everyone knows who Kristine is) was the clerical genius who kept the cases moving through the office. One day, while dropping off paperwork, I inquired about the stuffed wood duck perched high on a shelf in the office. Kristine rolled her eyes and said that it had been in the office for years. She told me it was "creepy," and that she wished it could be placed somewhere else. I joked—on many occasions over the years—that I would be glad to give it a home in my office.

I found out that the wood duck had somehow been the victim of a hunting accident. He had been shot—poached, really—by hunters who were later convicted of the crime. The duck had been lovingly preserved through the art of taxidermy and delivered to the District Attorney's office as a static, stoic, and staring memory of a job well done.

In 2009, I happened to be in the DA's office a few days before they were set to move out and into new quarters. That particular day, I was in the presence of Andrea, who is clerical, efficient, sarcastic, angry, and German. The stuffed American wood duck was still in the office, and for some reason was sitting on her desk. He was not the magnificent specimen that I had seen—even coveted—back in the early nineties. His sheen was no longer vibrant, he was covered with dust, and it appeared that whatever wire or rod had once proudly held him upright upon his driftwood base was broken. He had really become more of a bobblehead duck. I should note that his red glass eyes were also slightly askew.

I mentioned to Andrea, in a very serious manner, that I still wanted the duck. She looked at me with a sinister smile and fiery blue eyes. She grabbed the duck, dropped a few curse words, and said, "I hate the damned duck!" With that, Andrea tossed it into a gray steel trash can. He clanged as his driftwood base glanced off the rim when he dropped into the plastic-bag-lined abyss. I think the pressure of the big move was tough on Andrea, and the duck was merely a tool to vent her frustrations.

Any cop with even the most rudimentary knowledge of the United States Constitution—or any Mainer who likes to root around in roadside piles of discarded junk on garbage-pick-up Thursdays—knows that this was a "gimme." I quickly retrieved the duck and claimed him as my own. Andrea—in her staccato Berlin-esque delivery—said, "Take that damned duck, Cotton!" And that's just what I did.

The duck spent the next few years behind the scenes in my third-floor cubicle tucked in the back corner of the Criminal Investigation Division. He sat as proudly as a dilapidated duck can while perched on an Army-green filing cabinet, staring out the window with nothing but a sliver of a view of the mighty Penobscot River and the U-Haul truck rental and storage facility that blocked the rest of what could have been a very comforting panorama, to a duck.

He became somewhat famous at the department, as it was common to ask me why I had an old stuffed duck in my cubicle. For a time, he was called "The Duck of Truth." His presence broke the ice with more than one witness to a crime, as well as a few victims and suspects. The simple joke was that "you cannot lie in front of the duck." It worked, and even when it didn't, it gave me great pleasure to say it.

When I moved down the hall to take the job as a sergeant and public information officer, the duck came with me. In 2014, when the Bangor Maine Police Department Facebook page became marginally famous, so did the duck. After I strategically slipped the duck into photos of our officers and a few freelance shots around the city, people started messaging me and inquiring why we had a stuffed duck in our photos. I didn't answer them. It made sense to keep it mysterious.

I knew nothing about social media, but I knew that oddities could sometimes create a buzz; the duck did create a buzz. It was finally revealed to the public that the "Duck of Justice" had been pulled from retirement on my cabinet to become our page mascot.

The Duck of Justice moniker was selected because it seemed to roll easily off the tongue. It was made more interesting because any time someone mentioned "DOJ" on the internet, it would cause a few more people to investigate not only the Department of Justice, but also that duck up in Bangor, Maine. That was not intentional, but it continued to make me laugh, and in the end, using a duck as a mascot for a police agency is just plain funny.

When I offered up the chance for folks to stop in at the department to have a chance to take a selfie with the duck, we never expected it to become an interweb sensation. We were not set up for the onslaught of friendly folks who found it an appealing side trip on their way through Maine. The fame of the duck grew over time. Whenever the writing of the marginally famous page was mentioned, the Duck of Justice was typically used as the exclamation point. He has been featured nationally on the websites of *People* magazine, *The Washington Post*, National Public Radio, *The Huffington Post*, and the list has grown.

Eventually, things got to the point that tee shirts were created to satisfy the public's repeated requests for soft-plushies, keychains, and other DOJ memorabilia. We do sell the shirts, and the profits are channeled to community causes.

A couple of years ago, we had to refurbish the Duck of Justice. Years of human contact had caused more than his feathers to ruffle. He was rejuvenated and placed on permanent display in our Bangor Police Department museum. During his reclamation process, Ryan at North Rhodes Taxidermy and I had a few discussions regarding replacement versus repair of several of the duck's original body parts. I told him that the original duck needed to be preserved; I could not bear to look at him unless he was the exact same duck retrieved from the garbage. Ryan was able to take the decrepit taxidermy down to the bare bones and then meticulously rebuild the duck to fresh magnificence. He made me promise to keep the duck under glass from that point on. I agreed that it would be best for future visitors if the duck was in one piece when they arrived for their selfie with the World's Third Most Famous Duck.

Thousands of visitors stop by each year. They have come

from as far away as Europe, Australia, Canada, China, and every state in America; they continue to come.

The story has been shared many times on our Facebook page, but I simply explain it as a reflection of the opportunity for people to become better, even after sometimes being discarded. I think most folks can identify in some way with a forty-year-old duck who fell victim to a horrible accident, only to be recovered from a trash can by an aging detective soon after being tossed aside by an angry German girl at the District Attorney's office. Once the duck got back on his feet, he was able to find a place to call his own, and with his story of renewal—and maybe some magically manipulated hyperbole—he has been able to make thousands of folks continue to smile. Everyone deserves a second chance to shine.

1.

From the LT's Desk

A Pretty Good Day

I like the month of August. As a seasoned and sturdy Mainer, I can tell you that it might be the most perfect month.

The sometimes-excessive traffic that July brings us has thinned out a bit. The nights start to get a little cooler, and the mosquitos seem to have moved on after becoming bored with my blood type.

What is a pretty good day for a police officer? You have read the narratives about the worst day an officer can have, but what is a good day? I will give you some insight.

It starts with a sunbeam being chased by a cool breeze through the slightly opened bedroom window. No one else is up, and the extra-dark-roast Folgers smells stronger than normal. This is a good thing. Putting in that extra half scoop could border on genius. I would compare it to finding a faded and freshly washed five-dollar bill in the pocket of your favorite jeans. It was there all along; you just had to reach in one more time.

Even though the dog clearly indicated that she was in tremendous distress from holding back last night's hydration, she seems to be uninterested in doing the deed that needs to be done. You mention to her that she needs to do the "business," and she notices that the jogger going by the house needs extra motivation. After making threats of going inside, she looks at you as if to indicate that you tried that yesterday, and the day before. You wait. When she is satisfied that she has won, relief is imminent. Is she smiling? I think so.

The coffee is perfect; the bathroom is empty; and the hot water flows immediately without hesitation. The black-sock drawer is full, and your shoes are exactly where you left them.

The truck starts, and "Magic" Matt Alan must have read your mind as Jackson Browne's "That Girl Could Sing" comes on Sirius/XM 70s on 7. The only traffic on the road consists of those who are intent on getting to work by six. None of them dilly-dally. We all have someplace to be.

The parking lot is a decision-free paradise of empty spaces, and you get the one in the corner. No door dings today. This is shaping up nicely.

Your gear is where you left it; the sergeant is in a pretty good mood; and you get you first choice in cruiser, beat selection, and lunch time—the trifecta of a perfect day.

Your beat calls are minimal as the sun rises higher into the sky, and there were no burglaries of cars or homes—at least not on your beat. The night guy did a good job, probably patrolled the right spots at the right time. He left the car clean and full of gas. Someone pinch me. Am I being punk'd?

You check on the welfare of a woman who had not been heard from for a couple of days. Her family is worried. She answers the door, and you smell homemade muffins.

Her cell phone charger was chewed up by the dog, and she will get a new one today. You let her use your cellphone, and she makes the call. Everyone is relieved. The muffins were excellent. Houlton Farms butter made all the difference. She picked the blueberries herself. It is August, after all. She hugs you. It happens. It's good.

Next up is the report of a man lying in the bushes. There is no man in the bushes. It's an old, empty Jansport backpack—nothing in it. It smells really bad. You move on. You feel like the priest in the movie, *Caddyshack*, playing his perfect game in a lightning storm. Not becoming overconfident, you also recall that it was the priest's last game.

The D-beat guy is busy, and E-Beat is stuck on a traffic accident. Your beat remains quiet. Since you still have three bucks left on your Dunkin coffee card, you get an extra-large. No humidity today. The two-way radio is quiet, and it's double-shot Tuesday on K-100 FM. The Allman Brothers are up next. No one waves you down for directions, and you hear both songs uninterrupted. Man, you are so glad that no one has ever tried to remake "Sweet Melissa." As long as that Bieber kid doesn't do it.

Two traffic stops for minor violations allow you to warn the drivers to lighten up on the pedal and to get that inspection sticker taken care of. We understand that vacation with family takes precedence to our pesky inspection laws. The car would easily pass. Promises are made, and we all move on. Voluntary compliance is the epitome of a successful traffic program.

A counter complaint comes in, and you get called back to the station. These are like being last pick at a Yankee-swap party. Chances are you are going to be sorry. Not today.

The woman wants to report that she received a scam-call from an out of state phone number. She did not succumb to the promises of sudden riches. She just thought it might be important to tell someone about it. You thank her and advise her she did the right thing by blowing the signal whistle in the man's ear. Nice work, Mrs. Colvin, nice work.

Lunchtime comes, and the C-beat guy owes you pizza. No one is in the lunchroom watching the television and that means that no one is watching *The Price is Right*. Bob Barker was the king, and Drew Carey just doesn't hold the microphone correctly. Someone left a chocolate cream pie for everyone. You look up into the clouds through the window of the lunchroom—no sign of rain, no humidity. You hear the overhead intercom and the sweet voice of a dispatcher that you have a call pending. The A-beat guy calls in at the same time and says he will take the call since he knows you are eating. You remind yourself to buy him a coffee.

The afternoon run of back-to-back AC/DC is interrupted by the call of an active domestic on C-beat, and you head over to back up your brother. He bought pizza—it's the least you can, even if he hadn't bought the pizza.

The suspect struck his girlfriend with an empty glass and has taken off on-foot. He was last seen wearing a pair of baggy jeans and a blue hooded sweatshirt. Sure enough, he is walking quickly up Union Street, looking back in the opposite direction. As you pull up, he pays no mind to the man in the blue suit. You have somehow been enshrouded in the cloak of invisibility. "This is not the police officer you are looking for." You smile.

As you call out for him to stop, you have already warmed up to a jog. He looks twenty years younger than you—maybe nineteen, since you started the regimen of "Just for Men." No one has even noticed. Sure they haven't.

This will surprise him. Santa-cop for the delivery, moving in fast from the east. He hears you and does not heed your words. Strange. No one does anymore. No matter. You have a pretty good pace going, and you note that the baggy jeans are chafing him ever so gently. By the time he grabs his belt loops to avoid becoming a pant-less sprinter, you have taken him into a comfortable and nurturing embrace.

The grass is soft, and since he was in front, that places him on the bottom. Gravity and your extra fifty pounds are an evil mistress.

His pants soak up the inevitable grass stains, and your indigo-blue does not suffer even one late-season dandelion stain. The handcuffs slide on his sweaty wrists nicely. His knuckles are scuffed and bleeding slightly. He didn't just hit her with the shot glass. He calls you names. Note to self: Remember that one. It's kind of funny.

His mouth emits excessive noise, but it can be tough having an old guy take you to jail. You ask him if his mother knows he talks that way. He calls your mother naughty names. You assure him that she is a wonderful lady and that your mother would have caught him just as easily.

Silence never comes, even during his thorough search by the corrections officers. It's 1545 before the paperwork is finished. The C-beat guy owes you another pizza tomorrow. He is still speaking to the victim, who confirms that you have arrested her former boyfriend. You hope he stays "former," but you know things are not always that simple. The DV detective will follow-up further to help her get the resources she needs to stay away from Mr. Baggy-Pants. Hopefully he will stay in jail this time. Wish in one hand. Your uncle was right.

You turn in your paperwork and are changing into blue jeans and a ripped tee-shirt before 1600.

Little League tonight. Light traffic on the way home. Jackson Browne's "Running on Empty" comes on. You realize that tomorrow you get to do it all again.

It Wears You Down

The reports come in and are read in the order of arrival over the past twenty-four hours.

Wading daily through each and every report generated at our agency causes your eyes to blur and your heart to harden a little more.

I have found myself pushed further away from actual police work in the last few years. My good sergeant, who slogs through the opposite twelve hours of reports, was my partner in years past; still is. It is just different now.

We reflect on our wonderful years as "just detectives" sometimes in my office, late in the afternoon, when the sun is shining on our faces and our thinning hairlines. We both miss the chase, the mistakes, the wins, and the losses.

We miss the lies and the second guessing. We miss the slamming of a gavel and a jury walking out of a room to tell us that we pulled it off—again. We miss winning and the sobbing hugs from thankful victim's family members.

The good men and women who work for us now never knew

what we did or how we did it. They just have to trust that we know what we are doing when we prod them in one direction or another as they navigate the world of people doing bad things to one another.

His skill set in detecting was a little different than mine, and it worked quite well for us. His joke was always, "He does the words and I do the numbers."

He was referring to the fact that I forget things during long and drawn-out conversations with suspects. Our quarry varied; some of them guilty, some of them completely innocent.

He has a masterful grasp of details, facts, and a memory and level of intelligence that belies the goofy persona that he presents publicly.

My forté has always been just talking to people—mainly finding things we had in common, telling stories, and making them feel at home and comfortable.

I have a standard line that I share with younger officers. If you cannot find at least something to like about someone, even an evil sexual predator or murderer of another human, you will never be able to make them comfortable enough to tell you the truth about what they might have done.

I stand by it, and I have learned to find something to like about humans who did horrific things to others. My job is not to hate; my job is to get to the truth of the matter. In turn, and with an open mind, you learn to find traits in others that are admirable and interesting.

I was once put down as a job reference by a man who admitted to doing horrible things to other humans. Do you know why? Because he liked me and trusted me enough to tell me that he actually did do the things that he was accused of.

He then felt comfortable enough to put me down as a reference for a job that he applied for after he had served his sentence. I couldn't tell them how I knew him. I just called him and advised him that I would not be the person to share how we had met. He understood. I don't know if he got the job.

It's a strange relationship that is built between criminal minds and police officers' souls. You'd have to be there to understand it.

I know I take the long way around the barn to share something with you. I apologize for this. My mind does not work in a linear fashion, but I think this has helped me.

I need to take a drive, smell the air, and feel the story; it's just how I remember things.

One morning I was reading a report from a domestic situation between a man and a woman. While the officer was doing follow-up a day or so after the terrifying event, the victim's mother showed up to see her daughter.

Our cop was there checking the boxes, making sure she had what she needed, and doing the good work that goes unnoticed by the world.

It's not glamorous, but it's important. It won't be seen on *Live PD*, or *Cops*. It won't be seen on the *First 48* or *Court TV*. It's about crossing "T"s and dotting "I"s to make sure that whatever happened to them does not happen to them again.

The victim's mother showed up to bring her daughter a new doorknob and lockset to try to keep her daughter safe; to keep her daughter's partner out the next time he went on a rampage.

That's all her mom could do. In my world, that is not the kind of gift a mom should be bringing her daughter. It certainly says something about the human condition.

I don't know why that struck me. I don't know why I am telling you this, I really don't. But that's what we see, and this is what we do.

For a moment, just a few seconds, I disagreed with everything I just wrote about finding something to like about people who do bad things.

Like a continuous heating and cooling cycle in an engine,

furnace, or any kind of machinery, this stuff wears a person down.

Think about that for a minute the next time you see a cop go by with their blue lights and siren on. Think about that when you turn to your friend and say, "They must be late for coffee," or "They are headed to pick up the day-old doughnuts."

There is a good chance that that cop, that man or woman alone in a car, is heading to stop what that lockset and doorknob cannot. And we have to just keep on trying.

The Chair

During the last twenty-five years, I have found myself seated in the wooden chair more times than I can count. Last night, I decided that it should move with me into a new office. No one with any common sense would ever discard a chair like this.

I love this chair. It is far more comfortable than any modern, office-specific seating device, and I would hate to see it go the way of the gray military-surplus filing cabinets or the brick-shaped green Motorola "portable" radios that no longer transmit or receive.

The seat is contoured almost perfectly, the arms feel as if they rise to meet yours as you sit down, and the back is tolerable, even when wearing a gun belt.

When you are a police officer and are selected to fill an inside office-centric job, no one comes to you with a furniture catalog or swatches of fabric for easy drape selection. You use what is available, rummage around in storage closets, and take what you can get.

I could build a partition wall with the old Motorola's or an armored car with the surplus filing cabinets. Of course, we would never be able to get into the things as someone lost the keys to the locks in 1954.

I was lucky enough to gain control of the well-worn wooden chair because it was already in my office when I arrived.

I spent many moments sitting in it while speaking to the former occupants of the office—at least three sergeants during my time here, and, of course it has been well-used by visitors to my office for a little over three years.

I have never heard one person claim discomfort while spending time in the chair. I cannot say the same about a few uncomfortable conversations. I tend to stare a lot.

W.H. Gunlocke of Wayland, New York, produced this chair in the 1920s. How it became property of the Bangor Police Department is probably a boring story, but the stories the chair holds within its steam-bent arms are probably far more interesting than anything I could ever write.

I sat in this chair, or one of its office mates, during interviews to become a police officer. Several sister chairs were placed in the hallway near Sandra Russell's office in the old Bangor Police Department at 35 Court Street.

Good people waited for sad news in these chairs. That's what I see when I look at it. That's what I feel when I sit in it.

Some of the old wooden chairs, and probably this one, were placed beside the desks of detectives who did this job long before I did. Their questions, meant to elicit truths, likely created the smooth finish and polished patina that now makes the chair so comfortable. A suspect, under pressure, moves in ways that a craftsman's polisher never could.

Modern replacements with mood enhancing fabrics and powder-coated black-steel frames stand readily available for sitting at 240 Main Street, but I would choose this chair over all of those.

Ghosts sit in these chairs—ghosts of the craftsmen who built them, the criminals who lied in them, and the cops who cried in them.

I'll take this chair.

A Patrolman Pondering Parades

I like fireworks on the Fourth of July, but parades are overrated. This is the opinion of a man who has been officially deemed a curmudgeon by his family and all but several friends. I have been in, and directed traffic around, more Independence Day parades than I can count using all my fingers.

At this point in my career, if I don't have the day off, you can bet I will be posted at an intersection blocking traffic—an intersection where only people from out of state show up, all of them asking the exact same questions: "When will I be able to get through?" "How do I get to Bar Harbor?" "Why do you block Main Street for a parade?" "Our town no longer has parades, but we were sent here to ruin yours." "Was there a point in your career when you looked good in uniform?" Obviously, these people need to be directed back down I-95, as they are not getting into the spirit of the celebration.

The lead police cruiser in a parade is not a bad spot to be in. If the air conditioning is working and a little classic rock can be found on the radio; the driver's seat of a cruiser is the perfect

43

location for the celebration. It can be downright relaxing, as all you need to do is wave and go slowly enough not to lose the high-school band that is walking behind you. Waving to the thrum of "Won't Get Fooled Again" by The Who is a respite from giving directions and listening to donut jokes from the rowdy crowd of patriotic revelers.

Cops are usually lucky enough to be in the lead car in a parade, even before the grand marshal in the Mustang convertible. The grand marshal's ride should be equipped with an automatic transmission. Most of the available drivers are not well-versed in the nuances of the standard shift. No one wants to see the mayor topple backward onto the trunk lid—not good for the freshly waxed red paint, not good for his reelection efforts, not that bad for Facebook fodder. Facebook feeds are frequently filled with faux pas of the Fourth of July.

Leading a rural New England parade also gives you an opportunity to use all the modes of the siren intermittently. Dogs hate you, kids love you, and parents put up with it because it's the Fourth of July.

Inside the Police Interceptor, the siren is never loud enough to drown out Roger Daltrey. Windows must be up to shoulder height to keep the classic hits inside the car. This still leaves enough space for friendly waving to the kids. They can be very cute when they wave back. The majority of them do it with all their fingers. Hopefully you have treated the skateboarding public with enough respect that they only flip you the bird after dark and not at public events. Most parents still frown on this behavior, and their very presence causes many children to behave quite nicely.

Switching the siren into the hi-low mode (the British tone) just prior to Daltrey's scream creates a whole different experience inside the cruiser. No one else will appreciate the skill level required to time it perfectly. The kids will still be waving, and your smile will be ear to ear—a great way to celebrate the country's independence from the Brits.

By the time the last fire truck or ambulance passes, the sirens are getting a little old. The crowd's reaction becomes slightly less jovial. Nothing says "I love my country" more than crying golden retrievers and small children with their fingers stuck deep into their ears. Later, at the family picnic, when a mother asks Junior if he wants more corn on the cob, and the child says, "I don't have to go to the bathroom," you know there was a little too much siren and not enough John Phillips Sousa. I prefer "Stars and Stripes Forever" over any tone put out by a siren. Call me crazy, but that guy could really lead a brass band.

If you like classic cars, Independence Day parades usually have the best variety. Memorial Day is a little early to bring out the Gran Torino, and by Labor Day the alternator probably gave out, so the Ford is back in storage waiting for parts. July and sunny skies tend to bring out the best of the best.

Finding the staging area an hour or two prior to your town's parade is the perfect time to look over all the cars and speak to the owners. Typically, they love to talk about their vehicles. The air is filled with the cherry fragrance of Meguiars Quik Detailer and green, pine tree-shaped air fresheners. I love the smell of anal-retentive car ownership in the morning.

Try not to be the guy explaining why the owner is wrong about one or two particular details regarding their car. Yes, it came standard with the dimmer switch on the floor. Car owners don't want to talk to "that guy" any more than they like to explain to the town cop why their exhaust is not stock. Peruse the rides; enjoy the day.

So, take the kids to the parade. Around the age of twelve, they start to lose interest. Make sure that they know the universal signal for the drivers of the big rigs to blow their air horns. The up-and-down, left-arm yank is becoming a lost art. Is it even a feature on GTA 5?

If you take the time to slip in a couple of foam earplugs just prior to go-time, you too can smile during the parade, and your day will be far better. The kids don't need to know you are a curmudgeon. They are getting older and won't get fooled again.

Bobby from the Back Side of Brewer Lake

As I exited the plastic and portable palace purporting to be a potty after noting that a non-potable product was percolating from within its depths, I heard the strained voice of a metal-band fan.

I rubbed my hands together more vigorously to remove the recently deployed alcohol-infused disinfectant just in case the individual was calling out with a need for police assistance.

Wearing the uniform sometimes brings strange comments. You get used to it. I was an alien in their world of headbanging and fist-pumping to the driving beat of Halestorm. I could not make out the man's words.

He came closer. Did he mean to do me harm? Was he angry that I had intruded on his chosen listening post? Everyone knows that cops wreck everything fun.

I knew I was at a tactical disadvantage due to the magical potion being used to cleanse my hands from all that lurks inside of a polymer palace of poo. My paws were slippery, too slippery to engage this man, clad in a white sleeveless tee shirt. I noted that he had "kind eyes," and I made the decision to use only the verbal judo skills I had learned in a two-day class during my rookie year in law enforcement.

He spoke first, "Teeeeeeee-CEEEEEEE, my maaaaan!!!"

Did he know me? There was no way he could see my name tag in the fading light. "I love the Facebook page. I read it every day."

He seemed friendly.

He was also intuitive enough not to try to shake my hand as he had obviously seen where I was coming from.

I found out the man was "Bobby from the back side of Brewer Lake." He had a posse. They were enjoying the music of the Rise Above Festival—all metal, no excuses.

Bobby told me that his friends thought it odd that he was approaching a cop coming out of a porta-potty, but he saw me as friend, not foe. He asked for a photo; I complied.

His group seemed friendly, as well. We posed for several pictures. My "metal horns" seemed poorly presented in the subsequent photo, but I think it caught the spirit of the event nicely.

The Facebook page has landed me in some strange photos with wonderful people. These are folks who probably never would have even considered approaching a cop coming out of a porta-potty at a death-metal festival. It's nice to be among friends.

Grab life by the horns.

How to Act for the Media During a Snow Storm

Pretty much everyone in Maine experiences blizzard conditions occasionally and lesser snow events more regularly.

I could give you storm advice for days, but if you are from around here, you should already know all the tricks.

Since many people from outside of New England believe we all live like Eddie Albert and Eva Gabor in *Green Acres* (still one of my favorite television programs of all time), we need to keep up the charade.

In order to make ourselves more interesting to the summer people, they expect a certain level of Maine flavor when they see you being interviewed about upcoming winter storms. If you are interviewed by local or national media, here are some tips that I have employed in my not-so-successful career as a public information officer from Maine:

1. While being interviewed, make sure there is a shovel somewhere in the camera shot. People want to believe we always have a shovel. This, in turn, makes them feel bad-

ly for us, so when they return in the summer they will tip better at our local restaurants. If you are wearing a hat with flaps (and you should be), please make sure one flap is up and the other is down. The down flap should be on the side closest to the camera. Turn slowly to allow them to capture a Mainer in all your glory. By the end of the interview, viewers should be getting a glimpse of the upturned flap. They should be pointing and giggling. This makes them feel a kinship with you. Their emotional connection with you is similar to the warm feeling you get when you see a dog with one ear up and the other down. Better yet, have your dog nearby during your time with the media. His or her ears should also be displayed in a manner similar to your hat flaps. That's interweb gold, right there. Studies are rumored to possibly show that a single national interview like the one just described generates a higher percentage of tourists coming to Maine the following summer.

2. If it is not snowing at the time of the interview, ask them to come back in the middle of the storm. Do the interview in a sleeveless Carhartt hooded sweatshirt. Try not to shiver. Never allow outsiders to see you shiver. This will blow the entire plan. If you are asked whether you are cold or not, make sure you say, "Nah, this ain't bad." Practice the line to make it sound believable. We need them to seek you out next summer to take a selfie while they are standing next to you. You will be wicked famous as the person who was not cold.

3. If you do not have a red-and-black-plaid flapped hat or a dog, make sure you are standing near a woodpile. They love to see us near woodpiles. If you don't have a woodpile, do the interview in front of small pine trees. Shorter trees

make you appear taller. Carrying wood into the shed is also a prime photo opportunity. Walk slowly if cameras are in the area. Remember, don't shiver. Pretend that you have a bad splinter in your thumb. Magic. Just magic.

4. Whenever you speak about how you are going to get through the storm, please, please, please use the term "Mother" when referring to your wife, girlfriend, or mother. Things like, "Mother (pronounced Mutha) is cookin' beans," or "Mother (pronounced Mutha) is fillin' the tub in case the well-pump goes out," will guarantee a plethora of summer-types showing up in July. They want the flavor. Give them what they want. Do it for Maine. Do it for America.

5. If you are a lady, you should refer to men as "the men-folk," or "father." Please pronounce the word "father" as "fah-thah." You already know this. If they ask where the men-folk are, explain that they are in the woodshed, at the corner store, out in the garage, or at L.L.Bean.

If we all do our part, the summer tourist season will be bigger than ever.

On a serious note, make sure that your woodbox is filled, generators are serviced and ready, fuel tanks have plenty with some reserve, and anything that can blow away is secured so that it doesn't.

Check on your neighbors, especially if they are homebound or elderly. Let them know that you will be around, and you will be checking with them. Make sure they have your phone number, a flashlight, and a way to keep warm if the power goes out.

Candles are handy, but can also be a fire hazard if not watched carefully. I am not going to become Fire Marshal Tim, but please be cautious.

Cars should already have snow tires, a snow brush, a few blankets, a little extra water in containers that do not break if the temperatures cause it to freeze (it will), a full tank of gas, a couple of warm hats, and some really good gloves to make a night in the car just as warm as a night in the car. It would suck, but you can easily get through it if you are prepared. Clear the exhaust pipe if forced to sit in a running motor vehicle. Death is a side effect of carbon monoxide build-up. Crack a window, be careful.

Do not run generators inside. People die each and every year from being overcome by the exhaust fumes.

Generator? Outside. You? Inside. Simple.

Call us if you need anything. We do more than investigate crimes. We are here for the community and are willing to serve you in your time of need. We do not have flap-hats, but I am working on it with the chief.

We will be here.

Trudging

I really didn't need to be there. Watching the detectives of the Bangor Police Department work a case can be inspiring. They work hard, treat people fairly, and they get to the bottom of some pretty good cases. While in theory they work for me, they really work for you. I just watch them to make sure they don't make the same mistakes I made when I was a doing the same job.

I was riding with their sergeant at the end of a long day; he owed me a coffee and had finally decided to pay up. We stopped by the address where "the boys" had signed off in order to observe them in their natural habitat. They were executing a search warrant and looking for evidence to bring a case to closure. They found exactly what they were looking for.

They usually do.

They did not need me to look over their shoulders while they collected the evidence, so I retired to a central location of the home and decided to hold a conversation with a young man who had nothing to do with the alleged crime; but he was there killing time, so I decided to talk to him. I get bored easily.

It takes a while to get through the outer shell of a person, especially when you are burdened with the cop starter kit (a gun, badge, and notebook).

After a few minutes, he determined that I only wanted to talk for no other reason than I was interested in his past, present, and future. He had come down a long and hard road. He was in his early twenties and had moved many times, been to jail for a few minor things, and he was here in the city to try again. Most of his trips had involved trudging.

We've all been there, but maybe not right at the end of our rope. When that rope is frayed, it is pretty hard to hold onto. He was near the end of his rope, but he was still trying. I liked that spirit.

I do my very best to avoid judgmental statements with people in this young man's position. I just try to listen for something we can both agree on and then expand to something good about that. I am not professionally trained in the science or art of psychology, but I do know people. I didn't care if he had a warrant, I asked if he was getting food and finding any help in his search for sobriety from his addictions. I made some suggestions and tried to stay positive.

I asked him this: What do you see yourself doing when you get all of this under control? What kind of job do you dream about?

When the young man said, "Maybe I could wash dishes," my heart sank a little. There are times it feels like people are playing a medical game of Milton-Bradley's Battleship with my ticker and that was a direct hit.

There is nothing wrong with being a dishwasher or any other honest trade; my sadness came from the fact that it was his dream job to work as a dishwasher. We all have dreams, but his were not big enough. He didn't say he wanted to be the best dishwasher, a supervisor of dishwashers, or anything other than the dishwasher. This boy needed some dreams, even if he did become a dishwasher.

I had wanted to be a cop, sure. I'd also had dreams of running a huge successful company, building exquisite and fast automobiles to sell to discerning drivers, maybe becoming a successful author. I should note that I never wanted to become a police chief, and there is no hope of that.

I told him, in my own way, that I thought he was not dreaming big enough, and I felt he could do a little more when shooting for his dream career. He smiled and listened. We talked more about some strategies to get an education, and he told me he would look into them. I hope he does.

I gave him my name when I left, and I advised him that he could call me if he needed any more advice from an old guy.

I told him my name is easy to remember because it should be on the tag in all his tee shirts. I just said call the station, and ask for Cotton. Even if it isn't 100%, the name is usually an honorable mention on most tee shirts. He smirked.

He hasn't called. Lots of people have never called, but I would do my best if they did. All we can do is our best—even if it's washing dishes. There is no shame in that.

Pay attention this week. Someone out there might need a pep-talk. The good lord knows mine are not perfect, and yours probably won't be either. You just have to keep trying. There is no shame in that.

The Kid from the Trailer Park

His perpetually dirty face should not have been something to judge him by, but I did.

We do judge books by their covers. We are human, and we use whatever is easily seen to make our initial judgment calls and assumptions. If you say you never have, I won't call you a liar, but I will whisper to you in a private moment that I know better.

I only got to know the boy because he was always in trouble. There were plenty of other kids in town who I never met. They were probably behaving, eating regular meals, being driven to soccer practice, and not watching their father beat their mother.

In summer, I could depend on driving through his neighborhood and finding him hiding his hand behind his back to keep me from seeing the rock he was clutching. He might be riding his sister's bicycle, or any bicycle that he could find in a yard near the trailer his family lived in.

His sister was a pretty girl; a little older with a face that was always shiny clean. A smile attempted to smother her sadness.

She was smart and usually fighting with her little brother.

They would both walk up to my cruiser when they saw me drive through. I would flash the lights, honk the air horn, or thumb the siren, and they would lead their *Little Rascals* inspired groups from the tree line or from behind a shed to come talk to me.

We talked about what kids and cops talk about: school, staying out of trouble, behaving for the babysitter, and knowing about calling us if they needed help. They told me of things I didn't think kids should be dealing with, and I always tried to keep my facial expressions neutral to hide my surprise about the things they knew about and the experiences they'd had.

I would steer the conversations to happier things if I could. I dropped off a kickball that I'd picked up from the discount bin, but it was flat and lost high in a spruce tree within a couple of days. No matter, as a young cop you just keep trying to figure it all out.

The boy could not stay out of trouble. He was too small to cause major trouble, but he made up for that with the volume of issues he caused. It was a steady barrage of phone calls from neighbors and his parents. "Could you come talk to him?" He broke a window next door, or he stole some change from the neighbor's counter. He ran away frequently, and, while social service agencies were involved, he was not easily wrangled.

He tended to listen to me as I tried not to judge him but to enlighten him about the path he was choosing being the wrong one. I was a kid myself, maybe sixteen years older than him.

The day he tried to stab his sister while their parents were out was not surprising. He was dealt with through the system. He went to his counseling appointments, and I always asked if he was learning anything. He always said "Yes."

I finally made a deal with him. And like any deal with the devil, I knew it would not work out in the long term. I was naïve, and I had come to really like the kid with the dirty face.

I told him that if he could behave for a whole week, with no calls to the police about his behavior, I would stop by with a bag of Reese's Peanut Butter Cups, and he could have them all. I told him that he needed to share with all the kids in the neighborhood, but that it would be his job to pass them out. He looked over from the passenger seat of the 1987 Caprice Classic and agreed. We shook hands.

I drove through the neighborhood a couple of times that week. I asked if he was living up to the deal. He said he was. The other kids had been told about our Saturday plans, and they too had some skin in the game. They confirmed he was behaving.

Saturday came, and, while I was fairly sure that the boy might have cut all the phone lines in his little neighborhood, I picked up the bag of candy and drove through the park. He was waiting with all his friends, and he smiled proudly when I gave him the bag of peanut butter-filled graft. I shook his hand, and he made sure all the kids nearby were rewarded for his good behavior.

I told him that the plan could go on for years if he behaved. He agreed that he would, and I kept my promise a few more times over the course of that summer—not every week, but several. He was perfect for very short periods of time. When he wasn't perfect, he did it with zeal.

The boy ended up incarcerated several times through his high school years. He has ended up there some as an adult, too. His sister went through some very tough times, but, as an adult, she hugs me every time I see her, shows me pictures of her kids, and tells me she remembers my attempts at bribery and that her brother has talked about me many times.

Did I fix him? Nope. Did I try? Yeah, I think I did.

You should know that I didn't write this for you; I wrote it for me. I wrote it to make sure I remembered that you'll never fail if you don't try. We should all fail more. I believe we would all sleep a little better.

Think about that the next time you see a little kid with a dirty face.

The Italian Lady

In the early spring of 2014, I was still actively working as an investigator in the Criminal Investigation Division of the Bangor Police Department.

At that time, I was involved in the promotion process for a sergeant's position because, frankly, I felt like it might be time to move on to something else.

Believe me when I tell you that most of the skills you pick up as a twenty-five-year police officer do not translate well to other employment opportunities. How do you explain to your future employer that some of your best skills are in building temporary friendships with those who seek to harm children in order to help them admit to their wrongdoing so they can be sent to prison?

Do you then transition into your well-rehearsed explanation about your desire to work positively and constructively with others in order to increase profits and productivity at their widget plant?

To be perfectly honest, I had lost some of the purpose in moving forward as a fifty-something-year-old cop. I had lost much of the love for what I was doing. Working on child abuse cases, homicides, and other serious crimes does take a tad of the spunk out of you, and it tends to change you in significant ways.

Let's be honest, it changes you a whole lot.

Truthfully, it affects all police officers, no matter what job they are doing. You are more easily frustrated, and, sadly, people around you take notice. You become a little jaded, and, some days, it seems like you are still doing the job only because it is all you know how to do.

Successfully working an investigation does not automatically lead to a conviction. Many cases are not easily won, and it certainly takes a toll on an officer. Whether we like it or not, there are so many factors that are out of our control. Victims tend to focus their attention, angst, and anger directly at the police officer who they perceive did not do a thorough enough investigation to put the perpetrator behind bars.

In your life as a cop, you find that people are not always excited to see you, and even when the feeling is mutual, you have to continue to do the best you can do.

You have to look for the brighter days; this story is about one of them.

I was driving back from lunch in a white, unmarked Ford Crown Victoria. Cops drive them every day, but we sometimes forget how much they stand out and make us clearly recognizable. To us, it's just a car without markings or lights. To others, the car really does stand out as an unmarked cop car. It represents who is enclosed within the latched doors and dusty, smudged window-glass.

Even the cheap silver hubcaps scream, "The cops are here!"

I was wearing plain clothes: slacks, a dress shirt, and a nine-dollar tie from a discount rack of similar-quality, striped, polyester choking devices. I was sitting at an intersection waiting for the red light to change to green. The police department was within my view, right across the street.

My intention was to shoot across the street at the first flash of green, get back to my cubicle, and type one of several reports that were overdue. I could see it, right there, across the street. So close, yet so far away.

Just as the light turned green, a clueless pedestrian walked right out in front of me, forcing me to stay parked at the green signal in order to avoid a mishap with the slow moving figure. I exhaled slowly and loudly to indicate my frustration at not being able to do exactly what I wanted to do.

Who would have the gall to walk out in front of a cop car, against the signal, at an intersection?

I wanted to say something, but I immediately recognized the gait of a frail, elderly woman. She was carrying two bags of groceries. She was heavily burdened by the sacked cargo and was clearly winded, but she was impeding my forward progress.

I settled down for the wait as she was moving so very slowly. I knew I would have to miss this cycle and wait for the next.

To think she had the chutzpah to walk right in front of a cop car. Her eyes looked directly at mine. I could faintly hear a chorus of voices that included my mother, my grandmother, and my grandfather, urging me to get out of the car and help her: "She is struggling. Help that woman with those bags!"

Elena must have heard the voices, as well. She stopped, turned toward me in the middle of the road, and then walked slowly over to my car. As she came closer, she said, "Help me, pleeeaze. You da poleece!"

She was right; I was the "poleece." She knew, and she must have known that it had slipped my mind for a time.

The voice inside my head started in quickly. "Well, isn't that a swift kick in the rear end! How does she know I am the police?" The similar-toned counter-voice kicked in. "Of course she knows, you idiot. Do you remember those cheap hubcaps and oddly-placed antennas?"

I put the car in park and got out to help her. She immediately walked out into the opposite lane of travel. Cars were going by rapidly as they had the green signal on the other side of the intersection as well.

I gently grabbed her and guided her right into my driver's seat. I made her sit down. I asked if she was okay. She said she was so tired from walking so far to get her groceries. She asked me for a ride because she could not afford the price of a cab.

Her home was about two miles from the point where she had stopped my progress toward the safety of my comfortable cubicle.

Suddenly, I realized that I must have been sent here, by someone, to sit and ponder my own worthlessness and shameful laziness in order to provide this seventy-plus-year-old woman a ride to her home.

The inner voices kicked in again; there seemed to be additional participants beyond the original trio. "That's why the pizza took so long today. Get it? She's Italian!"

I recognized the accent. I had pizza. It all came together.

I asked if she felt that she needed medical care, and she said, "No sweetheart, just a ride." I will not try to mimic her accent in print because it wouldn't do it justice.

As we drove toward her home, we talked about her late husband and how proud she was to have sons in the military. She had moved here from Italy years ago, right after the war. She had a twin sister. She loves the "Po-leece." She wanted me to see her tiny apartment.

My cubicle, the reports, and my own selfish existence became completely insignificant. I eagerly walked her in. I was carrying her groceries as she fiddled with her keys to unlock and open the door to her tiny little world.

The walls were covered with black-and-white photos of Italy.

Photos of her sons in uniform were displayed proudly at eye level for a five-foot-no-inch woman who had impeded my forward progress.

She showed me news clippings of stories that referred to her boys, and a photo of her beloved sister.

The day, or at least those few moments of the day, had turned out to be the best day I'd had in years—at least as far as this job was concerned. I was there, by mistake, right when she needed me to be.

The officers pushing black-and-white patrol cars around the city get that feeling every day. I hadn't felt it in a very long time.

I stayed for about half an hour, and she gave me details. Some, I did not quite understand; it mattered not. She was going to have me over to cook spaghetti for lunch one day soon. I said I would come whenever she called, and I gave her a business card with my phone number.

She ran over to a small metal box and took out a packaged 100-lira coin minted in 1957. She had just returned from Italy on a trip to see her sister and family. She told me that she felt certain it would be her last trip there. I tried to refuse it, but she became very upset and tears welled-up in her eyes.

She said, "Memory! I want you to have this." Against my better judgement, I accepted it. I keep it in the top drawer of my desk now.

A few months later, I stopped in with my former partner from detectives to see Elena. She gave me a strong, warm hug after she looked at me for a few minutes. It took her some time to remember where we had met. I was in uniform this time.

She showed me the pictures again. She said she has a hard time sleeping at night. She told me that her twin sister had lost her husband to the same disease that had taken her own husband years ago. She explained to me the connections that twins have.

We stayed about twenty minutes. She tried to give me a map

of Italy. I had to physically stop her from taking it off the wall where it had yellowed with time. She laughed.

I told her we just wanted to see how she was doing. She kissed and hugged us goodbye.

Little does Elena know that she might have saved me from doing something stupid that day. I cannot say for sure that she kept me from leaving this job; maybe I would have cleared my head another way. Certainly she was able to knock some of the sour, self-centeredness out of me by walking out into traffic on her way home with two heavy bags of groceries. I just don't know.

Elena, the little Italian lady, let me know I was "Da Poleece," and I had better act like it, even when I didn't really feel like it.

Sad Stories

We could talk all night about the sad stories, but we don't.

I think all cops carry a bucket filled with sad stories. Some leave it their locker, or at least they think they leave it in their locker. Some carry it home with them and then examine the contents when no one is around.

Long-time cops have a few cracked seams in their dented and galvanized pails. The looped wire handle squeaks when they carry it, and some have a very slow leak.

Allowing it to seep out keeps it from running over at the wrong time or in the wrong place.

The bucket can be emptied from time to time. The faceless and nameless stories are shared with someone close to them. Shoulders are shrugged as if to say, "That's all I got," while their spouse or significant other takes it all in, nods as if to understand, and then skillfully changes the mood by moving on to something else.

No bucket can remain full all the time. Space must be made for more. And there will always be more.

It takes a lot to be the spouse of a cop— knowing when to be silent and listen, knowing when to change the subject, and knowing when to share some feedback.

This is just a thank-you to mine, to yours, to his, and to hers. Your jobs might be the hardest to learn, toughest to take, and most difficult to master. There is no college course or online training program; it is always on-the-job training.

That's all I got.

The Perfectly Parted Police Pants

There are some days when there is just nothing of substance to write about. On one of those days, I came across a social media post in which one of our officers comically shared that he had been having some trouble with the fitment of a few pairs of his police-issued uniform pants. He had found that the nether regions of the pants were not staying together.

I commented on his post that he probably had been ordering his pants in a size that was too small for his stature. Then I took a screenshot of the pants and shared it on our police page, with this caption:

These police pants were probably well past their prime when they parted in a manner perpendicular to the pavement.

It is also possible that the pants were parallel to the pavement when the participant pursued the perp.

Even pants can lose their patience when the primary occupant partakes in pastry as a principal prescription.

Perchance the Po-Po previously became perplexed by the

pantaloons no longer possessing a certain "stretchy pliability" for the portly party pressing against the panels of the polyester pant-shaped prison.

Perhaps he had used a partner to pull the pants on prior to this painful one-act play.

Previous patches could not stop the pants' penchant to peel.

Personally, I am pessimistic that these pants will patrol near the mighty Penobscot ever again.

Pity.

Prepare to pitch them into the pile with all the others that preceded them. Praying that they proudly take their place in police-pant purgatory, patrolling the streets of gold.

Schmidt and Chesley

She couldn't believe she was here. Four years of college, a really good marriage, a chance at a full-time teaching position, and yet here she was. Tomorrow night she would not be riding with Schmidt anymore.

Released from her field training officer a little early, she was finally going to be on her own, in her own car. Sweet freedom. Grouchy Officer Schmidt would no longer complain about the odor of vanilla in his cruiser. She learned quickly that smelling like a vanilla bean would bring the wrath of the midnight crew upon her, and it would elicit compliments from what seemed to be every drunk moron in the city.

"You smell *soooooo gooooooood*," was the last straw. The man reeked of peppermint, Pabst, Polo, and pine tree air fresheners. He wore an expensive-looking watch, had too much "product" in his thinning hair, and he hit on her all the way to the jail.

Schmidt just smirked as he drove; he would have stepped in sooner, but he wanted her to feel the pressure. It would be far worse when he was not in the car, so he pretended he wasn't. Other than driving and taking care of the increasing radio traffic from the squawking Motorola, he was a ghost only observing how she handled the idiot behind their seats. The cage kept the commentary muffled, but the man, struggling with his impending fifties, was one loud piece of work.

Drunks hear themselves differently than the sober do. It's very unfortunate for the sober. Schmidt wanted to tell the guy to shut up, but he didn't. His chivalry needed to be dead for the fifteen-minute trip to the jail.

Schmidt made sure that the in-car recorder was still running. It was Chesley's last night on field training, and he felt that a recording of the trip would be just the kind of parting gift that she could use as a keepsake of their time together.

He also planned to buy her a small coffee, because he was notoriously cheap—coffee and a keepsake. Like coffee with a cop, only with a video tape that was worthy of many viewings over her next twenty-five years here in the Queen City.

She had held her own over the last six months. She had her index finger broken, lost her radio at least three times, and inquired only twice about where the third-floor swimming pool was after an evil prankster put her up to it in the locker room. She caught on quicker than most. The kid, Frost, they released three weeks ago had actually brought fins and a diving mask to roll call. That was the beginning of the end—actually, it was the end of the end. Poor kid was gullible and was being eaten alive by both friend and foe. Frost was not cut out for the job. He would do well in his father's business, but not here.

Chesley hoped that her face was not showing the embarrassment she felt inside. No one had talked to her like that at school or even during college. This was a new level of obnoxious, but she had been trained well and was determined to just let it bounce off the dirty spit-shield and drop on the floor of the Explorer. The guy was an idiot and would regret all of this in the morning.

She looked over at Schmidt. Bathed in the green light of the dashboard, his smirk was showing. He never even looked over at her. He had been annoying, tough—kind when needed—but mostly tough on her. He made her drive to the E.R. the night she broke her finger. "I won't always be here, kid." He just looked out the passenger-side window as they rolled up to the hospital.

She was genuinely pissed when he told her he would be in the cafeteria having a coffee while they set her finger. He was a jerk. She understood, though. He did call her when she was on light-duty for three weeks. He told her that he was wondering when she would be back because she owed him three coffees, and he was sick of driving.

She smiled to herself; the drunk man's words had become like Nerf darts. She felt them, but they didn't hurt at all—not even a little bit.

As they walked the man into the jail, she noted that he had relieved himself of his excessive hydration. His khakis told a story he didn't realize was being broadcast to all he walked by.

She waited until she had his booking sheet completely filled out. She explained his court date, and he once again offered her his phone number.

She saw that the eyes of all the other future bunkmates were watching intently. Chesley looked down at his dampened drawers and said, at a perfect volume, "Oh, and all this time I thought you smelled like Polo."

The room fell silent, but only for a moment. The laughter of the others didn't fade until the door shut hard behind her. Schmidt's smile was infectious when it was in full bloom like that.

Schmidt sprung for a large coffee and a chocolate cruller that he insisted they split, as long as he got the larger "half." As they drove toward the station, she heard him mutter under his breath, "Polo, very funny."

Tomorrow night, she would be Schmidt's back-up, and they were both feeling okay about that.

We Don't Need No Stinking Badge Number

If you are a child of the '70s, '80s or '90s, you might be one to ask for a badge number when you are not happy with the service provided by a police officer. I get it. I have been asked for my badge number on a "number" of occasions.

It is very disappointing to me personally. I really would like a badge number. I have never had one at any agency I have ever worked for. Do you know how pleasurable it would be to spout out a hip digit like, BR549, 8675309, 2020, or even 54321? I am not going to tell you that I haven't done it. I am going to admit that none of those numbers would actually be my badge number. I just don't have one.

I also think that asking for a badge number in anger would be a fun thing to do—maybe throw in an expletive and punctuate it with a loud, "Now!" That would be great.

This particular phrase got its start, as all cool trends do, in California. Many agencies there, and in other places in the United States, issue their officers badge numbers. It makes sense that those who produced television shows in the past used this as an opportunity for value-added drama.

We do have a really big name tag. I cannot count the times that I would just point to my name tag. It is printed in yellow currently and is closest to a sans-serif font. It says, "Cotton." Maybe people thought I was wearing my shirt inside out. I have no idea.

People never believed that the name would be all you need to produce for a commanding officer if they wanted to make a complaint.

At my first agency, there were only eight of us. It seems that the chief always knew who they were talking about. I should add that he didn't always need to hear the name. He could figure it out when they said, "his badge number is 8675309."

Why do I tell you this? Just in case you feel the need to discuss a particular officer's behavior; you only need the name. We hope you don't have to make a complaint, but if you do, and the officer says he or she does not have a badge number, he or she is telling you the truth. If they are busy and you are yelling, "I want your name," please give them an opportunity to finish whatever they are doing, or just look at their name tag. It really is huge.

Currently the name tags on our daily-wear uniform are sewn on. The old "swapperoo" is much more difficult now. The swapperoo was easily mastered by taking an alternate name tag from the uniform shirt of an officer who might be off duty. This allowed a certain level of freedom in the way some officers might handle a complaint. It was never funny to the sergeants, but I do miss some of the hijinks from simpler times.

We know if you run into a Bangor Police Officer, you won't have any reason to complain. We have a very courteous crew. Some of us might have a bad day once in a while, as do you, but we try very hard to give you the service you deserve.

2.

If You Don't Like the Weather . . .

Dear Summer Visitors

We just want to let you know that we really enjoyed your company again this year. You always bring us joy and companionship that we would otherwise be forced to go without.

We cannot believe how much ice cream you ate.

After you left, we found 1,679 lone socks under hotel beds. Socks are not expensive, but, as true Mainers, we will be trying to mate them and put together 839 pairs. We will keep the other one in the back of the truck to use when we check the oil. You can slip it right over your hand as a thumb-less mitten, as well. We won't let them go to waste; handy to have when you scrape frost from the windshield.

Of course, we will have Mumma wash them. We are not completely without couth— whatever couth is.

Speaking of doing the wash, you people use a lot of towels. That sign on the counter in the bathroom indicating that you should leave the towel on the floor if you don't intend to use it again was really just for show. You can hang them up, and they will actually dry. You can use a towel all the way up to Saturday bath night.

Speaking of which, did you have any baked beans while you were here? If not, it's a darn good reason to return to peep at the leaves. They are changing color already. Don't worry; we know you won't stay around to help us rake, but a bean supper in the fall is worth the trip in itself.

About those directions you got from the man with the boots on. You know who I mean— green Dickies and a hat that matched the pants? He was the guy in the 1978 GMC pick-em-up truck with a homemade flatbed on the back. He had five milk crates bungie-corded to the bed. That was only because the guy from Hood Dairy took back the sixth crate when he was parked at the Hannaford. He was mad for a while.

Having an uneven number of milk crates does ruin the Feng Shui of the flatbed. We apologize that the directions were not that clear.

He knew what he was talking about. You just didn't know where the Gagnon farm burned down in 1973. It's not on Google Maps.

We know you found your way because he waited to see if you came back. He didn't wait that long, as Mumma had made biscuits. When Mumma makes the biscuits, a man in green Dickies will never hang around for very long.

We do hope you come back next year. Hopefully you felt we treated you right, and you never left a diner still hungry.

You guys sure do wear a lot of aftershave. You should try Bay Rum or Old Spice. You would fit in better. Remember, in a pinch, you can also grab a balsam fir air freshener at the cash register just before you pick up your lady friend.

Rub it vigorously upon your unshaven face and no one will

be the wiser. Make sure you wipe off the green flecks of scent prior to arriving at the door with the flowers you borrowed from the dumpster behind the florist's shop.

Always open the car door for the ladies, especially since the hinge pins are a little rusty and the door never shuts tight unless you "hold up on it" during the backswing.

We would love to have you back. Bring cash next time. Plastic is great, but we need the one-dollar bills for Friday night poker.

May your humorous Maine-themed tee shirts refrain from shrinking and your memories of our great state become more vivid in the coming year.

We will be here.

A Cardinal's Song and Mom's Blueberry Muffins

It's a standard morning routine, no different on a Saturday than any other day of the week. The time varies, of course. I don't have a visible clock near the bed, and my watch is too simple to have numbers that glow more than an hour or so beyond their last encounter with a light source. Nope, it's not digital.

I like to allow the sweeping second hand to smoothly pass the time. Sometimes I find it calming to look at it. I can't explain it, but it's true.

I have been gifted—at least I think it's a gift—with the ability to wake up at a predetermined time simply by contemplating that time, give or take ten minutes, just before going to bed.

I will readily admit that I set the phone alarm when I have an early flight or need to get on the road early on certain days.

I also know that my dog Ellie will wake me no later than 0445 and sometimes much earlier. The alarm never has a chance to go off, though; it's a backup. I shut it off before it plays the medley of odd little tones I selected as my personal tune. It's allegedly a warm and welcoming sound.

I stood in the backyard waiting for the pooch when the dawn light allowed me to catch a glimpse of a male cardinal landing on an all-but-bare branch of a maple.

As cardinals will do, he seemed able to stay in the shadow of the tree, so his silhouette was the giveaway. I wasn't gifted with the burst of color I was hoping for. My mom and dad always tell me when they have been able to lure in a cardinal, male or female, to the feeder by their window.

I watched, and hoped, he would fly to a tree to the east, where the sun was currently arguing with the slow-budding hardwood branches, but he didn't. I accepted my plight and crossed my fingers for a song rather than a full-showing, and he complied.

I thought about how there are so many conversations we get dragged into, all the while hoping for brevity. Yet the song of the cardinal never lasts long enough. I suppose if it was so common and never-ending, we wouldn't enjoy it nearly as much.

He only stayed for a few seconds, but it was a worthy wake-up alarm. He had other duties to fulfill, other people to please.

I usually only hear the cardinal's songs from behind the curtain of spruce boughs over on the property line. It was better than the coffee waiting for me on the counter.

My mom is out of town this weekend to visit one of her grandsons on a little getaway with my dad. Before she left, she violated some state criminal statutes by sneaking into my house and leaving me a plate of four oatmeal-flake-garnished blueberry muffins. She didn't leave a note, but I consider myself an intuitive detective.

If she were here, I would have told her about my early morning cardinal encounter. It would have been a good ice-breaker on Mother's Day.

I just consumed two of the blueberry muffins and they were delicious.

Chickadees

Our time here is limited; moderate temperatures and partly cloudy days would not make our storyline stand out.

I have spent time in moderate climates, and I long for drastic seasonal changes.

I was serving a fairly serious arrest warrant with a group of my co-workers about a month and a half ago; we were standing by and waiting. This job is far less about the excitement and much more about the waiting; don't let television fool you.

Being old, and sometimes being put in charge of such an event, I was a couple of layers back from the front-line officers who would be the first to swoop in and do the heavy, more dangerous lifting.

A snow squall came through and, with it, a group of seven or eight fall-mast-plumped and winter-plumed chickadees settled into a frost-bitten berry bush in a yard near my seat in the car.

I lowered my window so that I could hear their chatter and feel the snow and wind.

They flitted and nibbled, perched and pecked in defiance of the wind-driven flakes of snow.

While the radios blared, one with relevant information and the other with songs considered to be oldies, the black-capped birds happily picked away the remaining sparsely supplied and extremely shriveled berries.

When they did sit still, for only a moment, their feathers ruffled against the stiff wind. They tenaciously hung to the branches as the strength of their grip was tested by the sudden squall.

Our event went down without a hitch; a man was easily taken into custody about a half an hour later. I was pleased for the professional work, safely done, by excellent officers. However, my most vivid memory of the day was the chickadees—and the berries, the wind, snow, and cold.

Late that night, with the wind sailing by just outside my bedroom window, I fell asleep to a looped movie playing over and over in my mind.

Counting wind-blown chickadees is much more difficult than counting sheep.

This is a tough place to thrive, but that's what makes it most beautiful to me. If Maine were enveloped with moderate weather, instead of extremes, I don't think I would appreciate it in the same way.

So, while sitting still, waiting for moments that seem important, you too could be entertained by a wind-whipped storm of snowflakes and a small group of chickadees.

A Spring Night

April snow covers soft and muddy ground as the trees whisper their displeasure at the surprise fitting of a new spring jacket in simple white.

Boots find their way through the early evening coating of snow and discover dark and moist terra firma not far below the frozen precipitation

Soles re-enter the house with full intention of leaving their mark on throw rugs and recently mopped kitchen floors. No baggage claim ticket is needed as they drop their carry-on luggage wherever they please.

Dirty dog paws dig for lost sticks and twigs just below the surface. Whiskered and contorted snouts snort the odor of cold flakes and fresh earth as if a major discovery has been made. Brown eyes glance back with hope that you, too, see the value in the excavation.

Wet flakes land on thinning hair and stay just long enough to make proper notification that spring is merely one word in a long sentence of seasons that will come and go as they please.

March

The changing angle of the sunlight has been bringing me small jolts of joy over the last few days.

The uptick in the volume of sunlight between January and early March is but one small pleasantry that I try to focus on as winter wanes and spring teases.

Sunlight doesn't bounce off the surface of our snow-covered paradise so quickly when it is pointing down from a little higher position in our sky.

While I understand the science behind the change, I focus more on how it makes my face feel.

Sure, I discuss it here, but, if we find ourselves together in a sunbeam over the next month and a half, we should avoid chatting about the science and just sit still for a few moments and enjoy it silently together.

It is a good feeling.

Spring Moon

My eyes were drawn toward the moon last night. I refused to take a photo.

Clear skies over the 45th parallel guaranteed there was no escape from the fantastical display of the exquisite anti-terrestrial beacon.

I withdrew my inadequate electronic device from the pocket where it resides, cushioned, with loose change, small bills, and lint. I had every intention of snapping a photo so that I could later re-live the experience. Then, without so much as a click, touch, or squeeze of the button, I put it back.

I have taken hundreds of photos of the moon and none of them ever captured the magnificence that appears to my eye. Later, reviewing my work, the lack of depth, clarity, and context seem to minimize and subtract from the former vision burned into my memory.

I decided that I would just stare at it for a few minutes, and, to be honest, that was enough for me.

I knew the interweb would be abuzz with attempts at capturing the glory, and some would almost do it justice.

None of them will have captured exactly what I have secreted away.

There is no need for you to share your photos of the moon here. Sometimes we should just keep those to ourselves.

The Wind

The wind stopped by our town today. It never stays too long, and, while we all know where it's been, we never know, for sure, the final destination.

Groves of evergreens cause it to linger longer than the leafless hardwoods, but with no time for explanation, it heeds no hails from voices carried away by invisible strength.

Branches reach and pull back, empty handed, from their effort to slow the wind's progress.

Snow shovels, idle, fall, slide, and clang to the ground as if plucked from their precarious placement by the ghosts of snow squalls past.

Lids of barrels are lifted and dropped, while the lonely litter from within looks for a partner for the long journey ahead.

Old clapboarded homes with unseen cracks and crevices provide the instrument for it to play an eerie tune of whistles and howls as it announces both its arrival and departure.

Cold silence will follow; leaving us wondering when it will come again.

The wind stopped by our town today. It never stays too long, and while we all know where it's been, we never know, for sure, the final destination.

Peek-A-Boo

We talked about the weather warm-up as we played with our empty paper cups. Rejuvenated by the full-blown dose of magic bean juice, I rhythmically tapped the bottom of the cup lightly on the yellow tabletop. It echoed like the hooves of a tiny horse.

I suspect no horse had ever tapped his toes on that table. If he had, it wouldn't have been much more scarred and smudged than it already was. Tables tell stories, too.

Sammy said, "It's over."

I said, "Nope."

I knew he was talking about snow. He knew I disagreed.

The reason I knew this is because we are always discussing snow. It's more of a protection from the silent fear that we might have just run out of things to talk about.

Idle chatter usually leads to small wagers and forecasts based on what your uncle told you about March and April storms that came and went during his tenure on the earth. The confirmation is that any Mainer worth having a cup of coffee with has a story about sliding off the road because of slick spring snowstorms.

When the cups are empty and the conversation wanes, Mainers commonly argue about whether we've seen our last snow.

Again, I said, "Nope."

I played a distant game of peek-a-boo with a dark-haired little girl who had finished her chocolate doughnut. She was being slipped back into her white winter jacket by her dad. It took me three separate clown-level grins to finally make her smile back. It was only then that I knew the doughnut had been chocolate, as her tiny teeth tattled on the contents of her tummy.

I made the final tap on the table. You know the one. It signals that it's time to break away from the conversation and return to your chores and life after coffee.

My peek-a-boo partner, bundled up in a most excellent manner by a dad who had clearly done it before, looked back at me through the large glass windows that illuminated the public parlor with warm beams of sun. I waved at her one more time, overdoing it for effect.

Her hands were busy holding on to her dad, but her chocolate-coated smirk reassured me that she agreed with me.

No matter how hard we wave goodbye, winter doesn't wave back until she is good and ready. I think she will smirk a few more times. I'm usually right; all Mainers are.

If you're in Maine during March and April, expect a little snow.

Feng Shui Shoveling

Similar to a perfectly round pebble that remains unrevealed in the deepest recesses of your Red Wings until mid-hike, these small, steady, and unrelenting little snowstorms of three-to-five inches are becoming irksome.

You only need to shovel, throw, repeat; it's easier than following the clear and concise directions printed on the back of the Head and Shoulders bottle and aids you in accomplishing the task of getting rid of white flakes in short order.

Finding spots to properly place the piles allows you to actually utilize the knowledge you gained at that four-week, Tuesday and Thursday evening, 6:30 to 8:30 adult-education Feng Shui class you took with friends back in 2013.

Betty, who was angry about the fact that the instructor referred to it as a "pseudo-science," claims she hasn't tripped over the hassock since she began applying the Chinese principles to her family-room furniture layout. Why should you not move the piles to their perfect place?

I know what you are thinking, and it's cool:

"Hey, TC, why don't you take that shovel, remove the cracked handgrip, spray it with white lithium grease, and place it gently in a location where we won't have to see it again!"

That's what I like to see: channeling energy, removing the objects that could upset the balance, and using words as vehicles to rid yourself of negativity from within.

Good for you.

I am going out to shovel. Again.

February Note

February sunshine tickles the tips of the hardwoods outside my bay window.

I relish writing late at night, but I embrace the ability to write in the early morning. I watch the sunlight and shadows change between each glance out toward the naked maple tree that I use as a gauge of morning progression.

Like most folks, I have a favorite spot to sit when I am sequestered at home. A mediocre detective with little experience and no common sense could walk into my living room and make a quick determination regarding my favorite seat.

A pile of books, capless pens, wrinkled notepads, two re-purposed vintage Klipsch speakers (too big for the space), a two-week-old *Maine Sunday Telegram* newspaper, several pairs of quickly doffed shoes, and a pair of work boots are good evidence that "Tim has been here."

A green and chipped ceramic coffee mug, my favorite, sits precariously on a book about the history of Maine. I should take the mug to the sink and put the book back in the bookcase. I will, just give me a few minutes.

Two pocket knives, a broken flashlight, a tractor operator's manual, and a bent paperclip adorn the top of the old stand where I usually leave my computer when it needs a dose of voltage.

I don't even know where the paperclip came from. It is bent because I play with it when I am talking on the phone. I'll need it again.

It's not a neatly kept spot of space; I hear this from my significant other each time she arrives to find I haven't utilized the Swiffer or the vacuum as much as I promised I would.

It is a comfortable space.

The maple is illuminated in all of its gray-brown naked February glory. Warm rays begin to do their work of penetrating the icy driveway and crispy snowbanks. Soon the rays will come through the bay window and warm the hide of the black dog who knows exactly where it will shine first.

There is a worn and slightly faded spot on the rug. I see a green chew toy and a little bit of black hair that needs to be vacuumed, or at least Swiffer'd.

We all have our comfortable place. Even a mediocre detective with little experience and no common sense could walk in and make that determination.

The Breeze

This was written on a beautiful late autumn day while I was aiding a group of detectives in recovering a firearm used in a recent homicide. It was recovered, cloaked in an old wool sock, and buried under a log. It was a beautiful day, and these were my thoughts that filtered through the success and the ugliness of that day.

The breeze was filtered through pine and cedar. If you stood in just the right spot on the hillside, the sun struck your face in the most positive way. It warmed, but it also seemed to amplify the odors of the forest.

The only sounds were a lone songbird and the wind taking the long trip south. I have never taken the time to identify the chirps, peeps, and melodic tones of birds, but at that moment, I wished I had paid more attention to my grandfather. He took the time to tell me, but I was too young to even have the inclination to try to commit it all to memory.

Isn't it strange how, when we are trying to take something in—enjoying the silence, the moment, and the location—our minds still work hard to remind us of things we should have done better.

I decided that I wouldn't let my flaws ruin those few minutes. I committed it to memory so that later on when I could no longer stand, no longer be in that particular place, with those perfect conditions, I would remember clearly how it felt to just be there.

We should do more of that.

Early Onset of Darkness

The early onset of darkness over the greatest state in the nation puts me to bed earlier than I would like.

There was that time in life when staying up late was, for some reason, an honor.

Now, it's stupid.

If I had just taken advantage of all those naps my mother said were good for me, I bet I would have been far more successful.

By going to bed earlier, I am watching far less television than ever; yet I still pay the cable company about 1.29 million dollars a month to smash me directly in the face with programs that promise upcoming disaster just prior to the commercial break.

Upon the return to the regularly scheduled program, we always find everyone with all their limbs, no real damage to property, and we realize that the scream that was dubbed over the last scene is found to be someone yelling about receiving an acceptance letter to the college of their choice.

Yet, I still wait to see what happened. I am a sucker.

The down-side to the time change is that I am now getting up earlier than the dog. Today it was 0332.

She springs to life when my feet hit the floor. My set time for the coffee maker to start is 0445. I have found myself overriding the timer for the last three days. It's become a challenge to stare at it for a while, thinking that I don't need coffee until 0445. It's a lie. I press the biggest button and listen for the gurgle.

These are not trying events, just a few of the nuances of being alive. We need to embrace the little struggles.

I have friends who are being destroyed by depression, cancer, job loss, and heart attacks. So far today, I have it better.

Someday I will write about being on duty on a Christmas long, long ago when a dad died of a heart attack during the passing out of Christmas gifts—right in the middle of Christmas morning.

I sat with the family waiting for the hearse. Just a young cop who didn't have the right words to make it better, so I just sat and listened to them. Twinkling Christmas lights don't make an event like that any better—FYI.

They thanked me later for staying and just being there.

You can do that for someone today. Just be there. We don't always have coffee exactly when we want it, but we can listen.

Waking up on any morning is a gift. Waking up early should be celebrated.

January

January walked in like it owned the place and has been delivering on the expected promise of colder temperatures, more snow, and enough ice on the steps and walkways to fill Don Draper's highball glasses for the entire seven seasons of *Mad Men*.

Winter has officially arrived. He has introduced himself with a strong, cold, and curmudgeonly handshake to dark and wind-swayed evergreen boughs, ice encrusted lakes and streams, and our woodland critters, who had the foresight to put on their winter coats.

Winter for this Maine boy calls for more books to be read, snow to be shoveled, and the pleasure of viewing sunrises and sunsets that would cause a Florida sunset to blush from lack of depth and structure. Tonight was no exception.

Late-afternoon clearing skies just after a snowstorm create westerly views that laser their way into your memory like a first kiss on a late-fall hayride.

The hues of pink and red intertwined with rolling and rippling clouds on the horizon make you wish you could drive west forever while you cross your fingers on the steering wheel and hope the DJ has somehow read your mind and left the building after throwing in Van Morrison's greatest hits. He doesn't because he's too young to care about Van Morrison.

You are forced to hit scan on the radio dial and luck out when you find that Old Dominion is still producing the kind of lyrical miracles that make driving toward home an enjoyable slice of the darkness that covers you on a January evening in Maine.

Memories Never Have to be Exchanged

Pump the brakes, Blitzen. It won't be over until the fat man sings.

The most common question I heard around the halls and stairwells of BPD today was, "Do you have your shopping done yet?" Not one sorry soul said, "Yes."

I had to answer in the negative, as well. I am not even the least bit concerned. If I don't finish by Sunday, no one will give two Hershey's kisses or a squirt of peppermint.

Stuffing a stocking runs between thirty and sixty bucks, and that's only accomplished by purchasing some grapefruit or bowling balls to stuff in the toe. Does it matter? It really shouldn't.

We all say it's for the kids, but is it? If it was, I think the stress levels would drop like the thermometer in Fairbanks in January.

When I was a kid, I can remember some great Christmas gatherings each year—one at Grammie's, one at Nana and Grampa's, and one at our own house. As time flows on—and it does—I can recall but a few gifts. I do remember conversations, laughter, music, and the requisite Kodak slide show sometime in the evening.

I remember wet winter boots by the door and socks skidding across the kitchen floor when my grandfather made us maple syrup ice cream sundaes. I remember turkey sandwiches while we sat cross-legged on the living room floor and the family dogs tried to take their fair share of crumbs. They got plenty.

I remember my cousins, my sisters, aunts and uncles, and mom and dad; frost on the windows; and white, tight, starched sheets with impeccable hospital corners on a cot in the living room. Nana could make a bed that you had to slide yourself into like a letter into a tight envelope. Getting out was even more difficult because I was warm. Safe.

If you are heading to the mall to pick up one last thing, turn around. That one last thing will not matter in thirty years, not even a little.

Crank up the Christmas music, write a note to each of your kids, watch a movie, and make popcorn on top of the stove. Even if you burn it a little, the flavor will be a memory your kids will have forever.

Stuff doesn't make us happy. It never will.

Memories, people, hugs, and the slap of an old dog's tail—that's the stuff they don't have at the mall. You will never have to exchange it.

All we have is each other.

Valentine's Day Cards

Valentine's Day was a bizarre celebration if you were in grade school in the '60s and '70s.

I only remembered this morning about the decorated paper bag "mailboxes" we hung up in our classrooms in order to become the recipient of mandatory notes of adoration.

Along with the memory came the recollection that I hated doing it.

This event had to have been contrived by someone who sold greeting cards. It was like being stuck in a Hallmark re-education camp run by Mrs. Hutchinson, who probably deserved a Valentine's card—oh, and some breath mints.

Still, we forget—not our love for that significant special person—but to buy the card, send the flowers, say the sweet nothings.

If there was a life lesson in all that late-night card signing before the big day in fourth grade, it certainly slipped the mind of every man I stand shoulder-to-shoulder with in the CAOR (Crowded Aisle of Ruins) that is the Valentine's Day card section at every big-box pharmacy across this great nation.

We join the mass male exodus from office and garage bay, usually late in the day on the 14th of February, right after work, while we all look for the perfect card, which, by the way, was taken by one of the three guys in America who purchase a card well in advance of the "holiday."

Add to that a good dose of shameful price-gouging, which arrives with several shakes of cheap red glitter and an insincere message that can be recycled year after year on subsequent cards that cost $9.95 each.

Slipping a cellophane sleeve over the front of the card, in order to battle glitter-loss, adds another three bucks to an otherwise horrible poem.

Then we watch.

We watch her open her card. We smile and wait. We wait not for the hug, the kiss, the delighted look in her eye; we wait for her to casually glance at the back of the card as she wonders how much she was valued—just like we do when we get ours.

I sent flowers this year. It was far more expensive and nothing says "I love you" like $69 flowers which could have been purchased for $11.99 two days ago.

Yes, I added the unnecessary vase—red—so that the flowers can be displayed in order for others to believe I thought about this day far, far in advance.

I guess I did, in fourth grade; Mrs. Hutchinson, halitosis, become clear to me now.

I just want to let all the guys know I won't be in in the CAOR this year. You boys are on your own. I'll miss the camaraderie.

Truth be told, we should probably say the sweet nothings every day and skip the society-mandated, socially acceptable trip to the pharmacy today—only because you should have done it yesterday.

Happy Valentine's Day. Take your love to lunch, buy them a

coffee, and give them a call instead of a text. Do something nice. The card means nothing if you don't back it up with action.

But don't forget the card, because there is nothing we can do to save you if you do. Godspeed!

Autumn Lawn Care

Disappointment and dandelions are my go-to lawn ornaments.

My winter lawn-care routine includes pushing heaps of snow to locations that really should be better treated. My proximity to an actual paved road—something not all Mainers can include on their residential resumes—allows piles of residual road-snow to be plowed into the mouth of the driveway. From that point, I am to blame for the transportation toward grassy areas. On some winter days, that snow is measured in feet. Once it is pushed back away from the limited spots where one must drive and park, it tends to block the view from first-story windows.

Our parents tell us that when they were young, it always blocked second-floor windows. Most of that is hyperbole—but not all of it.

When the snow melts away to reveal the lawn beneath, usually by the third of July, the grass has been smothered for months. Add the fact that it has been peppered with snow piles infused with road salt and dehydrated cow urine and it is no wonder that grass is not all that excited about showing up on the fourth.

Of course, I am teasing about the snow's longevity, but, by the time it does melt away, the certified grouches in most regions of the country are already complaining about the pesky neighborhood kids walking on their lawns.

My landscaping routine is that I'll start to mow the more resilient blades of grass in hopes that the lawn comes back before a dry spell kills it again.

I don't treat the lawn with magical potions or chemicals because I'm not all that excited about mowing. I just don't want to hear the neighbors complain about the lawn-care slug next door.

Usually by mid-July, the grass looks reasonable from a distance; that's all I am really shooting for.

My issue now is that late summer's cool nights and sunny days, coupled with a full table of groundwater, have reignited the desire of my grass to grow.

I can actually hear it growing. From now until the first heavy frost, my grass will grow so thick and fast that I might have to commit the grass mowing team to two-a-days. I am disheartened.

There are other things to do in the fall; this includes raking the leaves regularly so that the maples, oaks, and birches feel comfortable relieving themselves of more of the same.

Mowing leaves and grass together as they intermingle in the backyard is just something more for me to complain about. Throw a fall rain into the mix, and you spend more time scraping off the nether regions of the John Deere than he feels is appropriate. While nothing runs like a Deere, there is no need to make him turn red from embarrassment. The neighbors will talk.

For now, I am ahead of the game, as I am mowing with the deck-level set on "burnish the soil until you can see the roof of hell" so that I can ignore the rampant growth for a few extra days.

Oddly, it starts to look exactly like it did once the snow melted away in the spring.

Where are those kids who ruin the lawn while trampling it with storming sneakers and flapping flip-flops? I need to host some flag football games and sell the soil rights to a lad who wants to dig some earthworms.

I promise to never yell at them again.

I Drove North Last Night

While east is my favorite direction, and Horace Greeley made heading west a "must-go" event, I drove north last night.

I had a couple of good reasons, but those are not important. I decided to make an attempt to meet my son—on patrol somewhere north of Millinocket—with the intention of buying him dinner at some place with mismatched tables and hot coffee, but he was busy.

He was busy eating his dinner, parked on an Interstate highway crossover, somewhere between the terminus of my trip and the Canadian border. We decided that we would not be able to get to the same place at the same time, as he had a few things going on and he didn't want me to waste my time going further north.

Cops eat dinner in their cars—more than we like to—but it's a quiet spot where we control the background music. Well, we control most of the background music. There are many times when dispatchers control the volume and selection of music on the crime-driven ambiance machine.

We caught up by cell phone, and we didn't talk about cop-stuff. We talked about whether he had spoken to his mother recently, how far his baby girl can walk now, and about how much the leaves had turned toward the shades of autumn already. We both revel in the color of Maine in the fall.

Unlike the foliage forecasts that show up in percentages on local television, we talked about swamp maples in red and his desire to wake up inside his tent this weekend, somewhere north of where we were now.

He was fifty miles north of my north, but we were still together in the magical way that technology allows us to catch up in real time.

We discussed motorcycles, fly fishing on the Roach River, and how I figured the temperature of his nose will be a good alarm clock when the tingling of cold stings him from his slumber as he attempts to sleep-in this weekend. Thirty-two degrees comes early.

We were both blessed, by my grandfather, with a nose that defies and rejects the warm coverage that the top edge of a sleeping bag can provide. Our beaks always seem to be projecting out of the fleece lining, alone, in the cold.

The gift of such a device is our ability to smell the sour scent of the fallen poplar leaves from a distance. This, in turn, lets us know that there might be a ruffed grouse, or six, rooting around in the mushrooms that thrive in the soil made rich by the fallen leaves of years gone by.

The smell of discarded poplar leaves in the fall is distinct and pungent. On a cool, sunny morning, with the breeze just right, it grabs your attention to let you know that you are in the middle of another fall. And it makes you count backward and forward to determine how many you have had, and sadly, how many you have left.

I told him to be careful and that I loved him. Only because

there are more important things to do than just driving north on a Wednesday evening in the autumn, I turned around and headed south.

Four points on a compass covered: Two in thought, two in deed—one phone call, and the start of another autumn in Maine.

3.

Thoughts from the Dooryard

Down on Elm Street

It wasn't a well-planned excursion; it was more of a side trip. If you are keeping notes, I relish side trips, conversations about off-topic subjects, and generally killing time when I should be more focused on the task at hand.

All of my former teachers referred to it as "daydreaming." Some of them phoned my parents or sent notes home, and more than once became frustrated with my extreme commitment to my laissez-faire trip through life. Even now, I have almost forgotten what I was about to tell you.

Yesterday, while I was driving my traveling companions through a small town that holds much of my genetic code, I remembered living in a house on Elm Street. There are lots of Elm Streets in America, and I was lucky enough to have lived on one of them—Elm Street, U.S.A.

To the best of my recollection, I had not been by the huge old Victorian house since the late '60s. I recalled the muted tones of brown and tan, an enormous sitting porch on the front of the home, and being outside with my mother while I jumped into piles of crispy, wind-driven elm leaves. It was probably a fall day in '66 or '67.

I found three houses in proximity to my memory. Each home had a feature that seemed familiar, but I could not pinpoint the house. I had no recollection of the street number that was screwed to the porch posts of the home. This clearly points out that my eye for detail is sometimes overpowered by smells, sounds, and foggy memories.

I remembered sneaking downstairs to hide behind a tattered brown recliner while my parents watched *The Tonight Show* on NBC. They never knew I was there.

I only stayed for a few minutes, but that must have been the first time I watched a monologue from Johnny Carson. By the way, Johnny is one of the few television stars I wish I could watch again. Maybe it's because of my late-night foray into the living room, or maybe it's because he was funny without being malicious.

I remember walking across the river to my grandmother's house via the railroad trestle while holding my mother's hand. I was terrified, but that was the shortcut. Remember, we didn't have bicycle helmets in the '60s either. I am sure it was safer than it appeared, or my mother would not have taken me that way.

I remember a blue Tupperware cup (with a snap-on lid) containing chocolate milk, and a paper bag that held a peanut butter sandwich. I consumed them both at a kitchen table after my walk across the railroad trestle. I recall, clearly, my beautiful grandmother's kind smile as she lit up a cigarette and moved her coffee and ashtray to the other room so I could eat without being bothered by the smoke that ultimately caused her death at a very young age.

I shook off the recollections and turned around in the parking lot of the Elm Street School. I think my older sisters had gone there, but I did not. I had no memories of being queried about being a lackadaisical student at that location.

I turned up the radio, and my passengers and I all returned to the same sheet of music for the rest of our journey.

Does this have anything to do with police work? Nope. It is only a reminder to you to slow down and recall the times and places that formed who you are today.

We all spend time rushing from one thing to another, making lists, getting to meetings, and skipping by things that might later become a darn good memory.

Don't let life get in the way of life.

Mopping the Morgue and a
Good Breakfast at Martha's Diner

*Tim, thank the customer when they check out at your register. Smile
and say, "Thank you for coming in!" We want you to do that every time
someone makes a purchase with us. It's important that they feel that we
appreciate their business.*
—Darryl (McDonald's restaurant manager) September 1979

I did as Darryl said; he was my boss. I didn't think much of it. I
was being paid to be there, and I needed to put gas in my 1974
Plymouth, so I did as he asked. I actually loved that job. I had
spent the summer before working in the housekeeping department of a local hospital. This new job was a cake-walk with a side
of French fries. It was a huge bonus that I no longer had to mop
the floor of the morgue.

I whistled a lot while mopping the morgue, probably because
I had watched too many Abbot and Costello movies. I can now
admit that whistling didn't help at all. Looking back, I think I

could have been more thorough. There were no complaints from those customers.

I moved from the McDonald's grill to the cash register, not because I wanted to, but because it would allow me to pick up extra shifts when my school schedule allowed it. Gas was 89 cents a gallon, and, at $2.35 an hour, I wasn't topping it off every time. Still, I appreciated the job, and I think I looked pretty darn good in the paper hat.

I still frequently say, "Got time to lean, got time to clean." I know the grammar is not up to par, but the slogan is tattooed on my soul. That was the idea. Mickey Dee's was all about keeping the place clean, and, while you were working, they expected you to be . . . well . . . working.

Now, you are wondering why I am telling you this.

I have been griping over the last couple of years to anyone who would listen that clerks don't say "thank you" to customers anymore. I have found myself saying "thank you" to them; typically they say nothing back, but at times they say, "You're welcome."

What kind of Joe-Jeezly response is that? It's supposed to be the other way around. It's the COD (Code of Darryl).

I guess I don't need to be thanked for my business; it's probably just me being old and grouchy, but it feels good to be thanked, even for buying a pack of Orbit and a bottle of off-brand spring water.

One day on my way to the sunrise county in far eastern Maine, I stopped for an omelet at Martha's Diner in Ellsworth. The food was great; the coffee was excellent; the service was fast and friendly; and the owner appreciated my business. Do you know how I found out?

He told me.

Our conversation went something like this:

Hardworking owner walks to cash register from kitchen after

pounding out fantastic breakfasts all morning: "How was every-thing?"

TC: "It was great, just like I thought it would be; that's why I came here in the first place."

Hardworking owner: "Well, thank you for coming here, and thank you for saying that; it means a lot to me."

The thing is, he looked me right in the eye. I felt completely convinced that he meant every word he said. He smiled. I smiled.

The words, "It means a lot to me" might be the best re-sponse that we can give anyone. And here I was just wanting to be thanked every now and then!

More valuable than a wink, way better than a shove, and, in reality, those six words are pretty special. It makes the recipient feel like they have really pulled something off.

I tipped well and exited the glass doors into a very frosty Sunday morning. The sun was shining directly on my face.

Ever notice how wonderful the sun feels on your face? Cold air, warm sun, good breakfast, a thankful owner, an excellent serv-er, plenty of coffee—and, might I recommend the Swiss cheese and corned beef omelet with homemade oatmeal toast?

It's really no big thing. Not much to write about, either. But, if you knew me, and someday we will probably meet, you'll find out that it doesn't take much to please me.

Didn't Even See Him

I stood in the lobby of the arena and watched the people saunter by. It is a position that I have been in on numerous occasions over the years. It was a beautiful day, and I would be fibbing if I told you that I was happy to be there.

Seeing a police officer is reassuring to most people, though there certainly are some folks who do not feel that way. Overall, I think a law-enforcement presence at any large gathering is appreciated by most of the attendees.

This is how I justify it in my mind when I run into the few, the proud, and the loud. There is always a contingent of those who have had a bad experience, watched too many episodes of *The Shield*, or have another deep-seated reason to dislike representatives of a police agency. I can't fix that. I choose to ignore the carriers of those attitudes and do my best to treat all people well.

Some people smile. Some people try hard to avoid eye contact, and I understand that. That does not make me suspicious; it makes me believe that many people are shy, introverted, or have other things on their mind.

I think a police officer should be seen but avoid becoming part of the show unless conditions make it necessary.

I like to watch people and look for those who appear similar to more famous people, past and present. It forces me to pay attention to what people are up to and adds some entertainment for my simple mind.

If I am lucky enough to be close to another officer, I might point it out to them without being too obvious and take a quick poll on whether they agree with me. Usually they do. I am pretty good at that.

I have spent hours amusing myself while smiling kindly to people who look like Elvis, John Wayne, or Ricardo Montalban.

Last year at Reagan National Airport, I saw a man who I pointed out as looking exactly like Joseph Simmons from the band Run-DMC. Turned out he actually was Joseph Simmons. I told you I was pretty good at it.

This past weekend, I found my assigned position in the lobby of the building and began my search for those with "star qualities."

The man was discussing whether he could leave the venue and be able to get back in before the festivities got under way. He looked familiar, but I could not place him. He did not look like a star.

Dressed in dark clothing, with a short haircut and a weathered appearance, he was a person that spent time outdoors. I was sure of that.

I turned away and walked back to a wall where I could surreptitiously lean to give my feet a break from the concrete floor. I found a divine patch of old carpet that I could move to when my heels started to burn a little. Smart cops stand on carpet. Old cops do, too. I am not smart. You can figure out which kind of cop I am.

When he walked up to me, I knew in an instant who he was.

He had aged in the thirty-five years since I had last seen him this close. We'd had a post-high school disagreement that ended up becoming physical—yes, a fist fight, right in the driveway of a mutual friend's house.

Those were the days when friends got into a fist fight and no one called the police.

Typically, those fights ended up with black eyes, bloody noses, and a handshake accompanied by an apology. Ours ended with angry words and my friend driving off, giving me the finger and saying things I knew he didn't mean.

In the following years, we worked in the same industry after college. He was better at it than I was and did very well. Bright, smart, funny, engaging, and damaged—damaged by things that aren't mine to discuss, things that would break the strongest man's will and spirit.

He tried to work through it. He didn't do well. He turned to alcohol, and drinking excessively caused him to do things he thought he would never do.

At that moment in time, none of this mattered to me. I was glad to see him.

He asked me if I knew who he was, and I said, "Of course I do." I said his first name and we shook hands. I told him that I had been watching him a few minutes prior to our face-to-face and had thought to myself that he looked familiar. His smile was the same and his voice distinctive.

He said, "I thought you would pretend you didn't know me." I shook my head and scowled to indicate that the statement was ridiculous. He spoke of our last disagreement as if it had happened yesterday. I remembered it just as clearly, but I had let go of that beef within a week or two of his burnout up the Pushaw Road in Glenburn, Maine. He carried a lot of guilt and this was something that should have been thrown out of his pack years ago.

My friend then told me that he has been homeless for a

very long time. This summer he was living in the woods within a five-minute walk of my police department, and I knew nothing about it. If he had punched me directly in the face, it would have hurt far less.

My friend—the standout athlete with a middle-class upbringing, a college education, and a skill set that could have placed him far above all others in his field—was homeless.

Internally I cringed, but I tried to suppress my "surprised face."

I wanted our conversation to be normal stuff—the stuff I say to all my other long-lost friends after thirty-five years of no contact. How's the family? When are you going to retire? Where are your kids going to college? None of the standard questions applied. Instead, I just told him I was so sorry. I am not positive, but I think I might have said I was sorry at least two more times.

I am not a man who has ever been accused of being at a loss for words—but that changed when he told me.

I could smell the odor of intoxicants on his breath, and I could see that his eyes had the sheen of a man who spent much of his time near a bottle. He told me that he had a stash of alcohol hidden in the bushes outside the venue and that he was heading out the door to have a quick drink before coming back inside. He was headed for the door when we came face-to-face.

He told me of arrests and prison, that he was able to function enough to work every single day as a temporary employee, and that he had a bus ticket in his pocket to go back to Florida the very next day. He is a transient homeless man. He is a functioning alcoholic.

He likes Florida in the winter. We had that in common. We have more in common than most people do.

He made me laugh like he used to. When I asked him how living outdoors affects him, he told me, "Tim, Jesus was transient and slept outside every night. I am doing the same thing—not in the winter, mind you. I'll be in Florida while you are shoveling this winter." We both laughed at the absurdity of his reasoning. He was trying to make it easy for me. He did it well, covering his hurt with humor. I do it, too, but my hurt pales in comparison to his. He was a professional at making people around him feel better about his situation.

He showed me worn photographs of his children. He explained how, after all his child support payments are removed from his check, he has about thirty dollars a day left to live on. Much of that goes to alcohol; none of it goes to housing.

He has no license and refuses to get it reinstated, as he knows he would drink and drive again. "It's not worth it, Tim. I could kill someone if I was driving. I cannot live with that."

My friend showed me that he had plenty of traveling cash for the three-day bus trip to Florida and that he would be working a temporary job there as soon as he arrived. He shared that he would be back next summer and would be living in the same spot. He said he had a great campsite.

I told him to come to the station as soon as he arrived next summer, and we could catch up, grab a sandwich, and, if I could make his life better or easier, I would do what I could.

He said, "I am not looking for a handout. I get by. I'm just so glad I got to see you." I told him I was happy to see him, as well—so happy, and yet so sad.

Sad that my friend was living in the bushes within walking distance of where I ate my lunch every day. Sad that he didn't feel he could stop by and say hello because he surmised that I would not recognize or speak to him. Sad that we had not made up after a fight over something that I had forgotten about minutes after it happened.

This story is about all of us. It is about all of our unseen or forgotten friends and acquaintances. It is about saying you are sorry when something might not be your fault. It is about paying attention to other people and about knowing that you don't have to look too far to find someone in need.

Take a look out your window. I didn't.

The Kid

My nap was interrupted by the late-afternoon fog rolling up the lake from the Atlantic; the ocean was not far away if you didn't have to rely on pavement or crushed gravel to get there.

It wasn't the fog that woke me—fog is silent, welcome, and expected on the coast of Maine—it was the mist atomized by the twenty-year-old screens meant to protect me from mosquitos who wouldn't take "no" for an answer. The floating droplets wafted down gently to my face and was a far more pleasant alarm than any sound that ever emanated from a man-made device.

The Washington County, Maine contingent of PWTPIAPS (People Who Think Pie Is A Perfect Supper) was officially called to order. Camp weekend was coming to a close and my feet slamming to the floor of the porch awakened the only other charter member within several miles. I'll call him Dave, simply because that's his name. He had found the couch to his liking, and I knew he was awake because his snoring stopped abruptly.

I am embarrassed to declare that we had not come close to

finishing the work we had gone to camp to do, but the naps are mandatory, regardless of whether or not the list is complete. We had slipped into Lubec earlier that day to do some official fried-clam testing. The nap could have been a legitimate clam-coma, because Becky did not disappoint. I'll do further research at a later date.

I yelled into the cottage that we should skip supper and just take the ATV to Helen's for raspberry pie before it got too dark. More importantly, before the pie was sold out. He grunted and went looking for his shoes and a jacket to repel the heavy mist.

We were soaked before we got there. The good news is, if you sit at the bar, no one cares if your shirt is wet, and you don't have to wait in line. If you have ever been to Helen's, you already know how good the pie is. You also know how long the line for pie can be.

Full of pie, eastbound under darkening skies, and soaked again, we came across a young man who had run out of fuel and was standing beside his older Suzuki Quad (purchased for a righteous price from an older gentleman who no longer had a need for the conveyance. I am inquisitive in matters of importance).

We stopped because that's what you do in Maine. I asked him if he was out of gas, and, even though I already knew the answer, it's a heck of an icebreaker. He smiled and said, "I thought I had enough to get home." A handsome kid, he was wearing well-torn jeans, a dusty shirt, and, most notably, he was shoeless. He had taken off his helmet and was standing on coarse gravel that didn't seem to faze him a bit. I would have been doing a painful shuffle if standing on the same ground without my shoes.

I made a mental note to ask him about it if the opportunity presented itself. The six-inch sheathed hunting knife swinging from his belt didn't bother me a bit. I admired his preparedness. It's Maine; knives are as common as iPhones are in the places with better cell coverage. Remind me to tell you the story of getting my knife taken away at the Hoover Dam. That's a song for another time.

I had no gas can, and nothing to siphon a little from my tank, so I told him that Dave would get out and he could get in. I would drive him to the store and try to find a container to put fuel in when we arrived. I knew it was close to closing time.

I saw that he had an empty plastic soft drink bottle wedged in his front rack and told him to bring it, just in case. It was a good idea. The phrase "just in case" has saved me more times than I can count. It might be the best three-word sentence this side of "That was stupid," or "I shouldn't have."

Dave started walking in the direction of camp, and the kid and I drove back into East Machias. I asked him over the roar of the engine if he had a cap for the bottle. He said he didn't. I saw that he had thumbs and thought to myself it was the next best thing to a cap, and they were much easier to keep track of.

It was a short ride, and he could have easily walked it in ten minutes, but this is how it works.

After he filled the bottle with 15.9 ounces of fuel, he paid, stuck his thumb in the bottle, and we headed back to the trail.

I asked him where his shoes were. He said he doesn't wear them much in the summer. I asked if his feet hurt. He explained that once you go without shoes for a while, your feet become calloused, and they don't hurt a bit. I told him I never could get used to it, even when I was his age. He was fifteen; I had guessed a little older.

The kid told me he really liked the convenience of not having to put on shoes before he left the house as well as the amount of time he saves each day by not having to tie them. We both laughed. The kid had a good sense of humor, self, and direction.

I dropped him off, made sure his wheeler started, and headed east again. I couldn't help but think the kid had it pretty well figured out. Sure, he might have needed to be a better estimator of fuel mileage—or did he?

I picked up Dave about a mile down the trail, and he said other than the heavy mist, he felt a little better walking off the pie. I told him about the young man's answer regarding the shoes. Dave thought it made perfect sense.

In the simple everyday encounters, most of us picture ourselves as the person doing the helping, but I don't think that's always true.

As you go through life, it's always better to be awakened by a light mist on your face, skipping the entree and going straight for the raspberry cream pie, stopping when someone needs help, talking less, listening more, and not getting all worked up over unnecessary daily tasks. Those can be a waste of valuable time. Allowing ourselves to toughen up against the inevitable, and sometimes endless, onslaught of painful encounters might also be a takeaway.

The kid was a genius, and he barely said a thing. I never did get his name, but he would have told me if I needed to know.

My First Car

My first car was a 1974 Plymouth Satellite. I bought it used in the summer of 1979 from a fellow who was selling all his worldly possessions to become a missionary. I earned the money for that car working for a nun.

Looking back, I wish one of them would have said a prayer for all the voltage regulators that I went through over the next couple of years. I learned fast and kept a spare in the glove box.

There was no internet to check reliability ratings on an automobile. If there had been, I would not have cared. The car had a V8, two doors, and a bench seat. What more could a young man ask for? I had already learned that it really didn't matter what I asked for. I was told if I wanted wheels, I would have to work for them.

The $900 price tag was tough to come by at $2.35 an hour.

I spent the summer of my sixteenth year working in the housekeeping department of a Catholic hospital in my hometown. There were some special dispensations that were required for them to allow me to work in the hospital, or, as I told my chums, the medical field. None of the dispensations were among the original seven.

Mainly, I needed special permission from the State of Maine in order to be able to work forty hours per week. While I had reached the age of consent, the state still felt the need to oversee my formative years in the blue-collar sector. I applied for and received a work permit to make me a valuable member of the summer work force.

I showed up for work each morning at six o'clock in the most horrible way a young man can arrive at a job—being driven by my mother. She knew that dropping me off down the road from the employee entrance was a necessity to save me from the inevitable ridicule from the adult members of the housekeeping crew.

The thought of this being the last summer of my dependence on my parents for transportation helped me keep my eye on the prize.

A plain, tan Plymouth—the Cragar Super Sport wheels would have to come later. Those were not achievable on my current nonexistent budget.

The housekeeping crew was at that time overseen by a nun named Sister Mary F. (last name withheld for fear of reprisal upon entering the pearly gates). I learned during that summer that she was a tough Polish woman who had no time for hijinks. My wage was a pittance, and she made sure that I worked for every penny of it. If I even leaned on a mop, that woman would come out of nowhere and say things to me that seemed un-Christian; however, I was not positive of this as she yelled at me in her native tongue.

I had not taken Polish 101 during my freshman year; if I had, I might have been able to confirm that some of her words were not on the "approved list" at the Vatican. Was the Pope Polish? There was no way I would be asking her that question.

I recall one event that left a lasting impression and taught me to be more cautious when screwing around on the job, which in turn made me a better employee for future employers.

I had gone in to sweep and wet mop a room after a major renovation job. I don't remember what we were laughing about with the construction crew, but it was not funny to the woman behind me.

She inhabited a habit as well as the darkened and dirty bathroom.

She emerged with her angry face on, which was probably also her pleased face, as far as I could tell. Being sixteen, I made the assumption that she was unhappy. Being struck in the face with a dust cloth also led me to believe in her divine displeasure.

She yelled to me that I needed to "Cut out the shekanigans." I made the mistake of saying, "What?" Sister Mary F. again repeated the same sentence and I, in my emerging juvenile sarcasm phase, made the decision to build street cred with the construction crew. I asked her, "What is a 'shekanigan'?" That is when the balled-up cloth struck me directly in the face.

It did not hurt, but the construction crew laughed so loudly that I decided to go with a Tim Conway face and just stare blankly at the twisted sister.

I was raised to remain respectful to all elders, and, while not being Catholic, I still felt guilty. I realized that my summer would be made hellish by the sister, regardless of what I did in that moment. I also knew that I would be spending much more time with the construction crew as the rehab of the hospital continued for two more months.

Knowing that I would not be attending any confessionals in the hospital chapel, I decided that I needed the construction crew on my side if I were to make it through the summer and become "one of the boys."

I took a breath and said, "Ohhhh, you mean 'shenanigans'?" The sister's white shoes (late-'70s nursing style) began to pivot and suddenly stopped. The construction crew had become silent, and I felt very alone. The former dust-cloth-turned-Catholic-attention-getting device lay at my feet.

She told me to "Peek it up." In later years, I realized that Ren, from *Ren and Stimpy* fame sounded exactly like the Sister and made the adult cartoon so much more meaningful to me. It also gave me flashbacks. I never did seek help for this.

She held out her hand and I leaned over, fully expecting to be smacked on the head. She wanted to, I am positive. The pain never came. I picked up the rag and gingerly placed it into her rock-steady palm. With that, she turned and walked out of the room. I know that I did not win with the sister, but the construction crew remained silent as I finished mopping up the sheetrock dust.

Two things happened in that moment. I earned a small amount of respect from her by "peeking" up the cloth and placing it in her hand, and I was placed on her permanent naughty list.

This gave me more opportunity in my chosen field. I would find myself cleaning the morgue more often, and I was allowed to learn about how the sheets at the hospital became so clean—and crisp.

Being sixteen and funny in front of a construction crew is easy compared to walking down a dark corridor knowing that there was the possibility that I would be in a cold room with actual dead bodies. I never saw any, but I did not go through the drawers, if you know what I am saying. I was terrified each time I mopped that room. I am not sure that I did my best work there, especially after the mandatory knocking on the walls and deep-voice salutations that fellow crew members felt obliged to torment me with.

I was sent to the basement laundry more often to help the laundry supervisor "Shake-a-tha-sheets." Sadly, the laundry supervisor was the sister's brother. Yes, the sister's Polish brother ran the steaming-hot hospital laundry room. Charlie had no sense of humor. He watched me very carefully. There were no holidays in Charlie's laundry room. He had been there a long time. I just had to make it until the end of August.

It was evident to a neophyte sheet-shaker that Charlie had heard about me attempting to translate the word "shekanigans" into my native tongue. He was not amused and made sure that I did not take breaks from the shaking and folding and stacking of the steaming hot sheets, fresh out of the dryer.

The laundry room was in the basement, ridiculously hot, and there was no patience or time for hijinks. I won't lie to you. Since it was run by a tyrant of a man, I thought of it as an earthly representation of what hell would be like. I certainly was not sent there by an angel.

It is highly possible that Sister Mary F. was trying to tell me something.

I was raised to work for what you wanted, and, in some strange way, I have pleasant memories of those people and that experience.

I picked up the Plymouth about a week before I returned to my junior year in high school. The Audiovox FM converter was left in the car by the missionary—perhaps by mistake, but I like to think of it as a blessing.

Those things were about fifteen bucks. Doing the math, that equaled a little over six hours of "shekanigans."

Appreciating the Lack of Perfection

My appreciation for "less than perfect" is on the uptick. I find myself looking at old things in a new light.

My long-time friend, who pulled up stakes and moved off to Ohio a long, long time ago, told me in a phone conversation that one of his simple pleasures was being able to keep things long enough to wear them out. I think that is a worthy pursuit.

I also have decided to compliment people on the condition of their older property. People perk up when you notice the things that they take pride in.

The good news is that I roam, solo, quite often now that my number-one fan spends more time on the road. It leaves my itinerary quite open to those initially uncomfortable conversations with other introverts who merely need to be spoken to first.

Mainers are not all that flamboyant—FYI. Oh, they love to talk, but, in general, they are not always going to start the conversation. That's where I come in.

I was carrying a decrepit lawnmower battery across the back lot of an auto parts store last night, with intentions of getting a new one, when I saw a man standing beside a slightly rusted GMC pick-em-up truck. It was a late '70s "square body" with what appeared to be original paint.

I wasn't going to say anything to him, but I admired the vehicle for what had *not* been done to it. It was not pristine by show-car standards, but it was a survivor.

What's not to love about a survivor?

It took me about seven steps past the truck to make a smooth segue into conversation-mode, but I wanted to tell him I liked the truck.

I was carrying the greasy, dead power-cell in my right hand like a waiter bringing the second course to a white-cloth-covered round table in the corner of a posh eatery. I stopped, spun around, and said, "Man, I like your truck."

He looked surprised. I believe he looked surprised because his vehicle had a working truck's patina; it lacked any shine in the late-afternoon sun.

One of the gifts I have received in my years spent interviewing people, some of whom have done very bad things, is that I have overcome the fear of pushing words out of my mouth that might feel alien to other people.

These words were not uncomfortable, but they did surprise the man. He opened up like a broken faucet and told me he picked it up as a "parts truck" in North Carolina. He told me the price and that he hauled it home with a truck that was in much better condition.

He advised me that he decided to turn the other truck into a "mud truck," and this one is now his daily driver. It was a '79.

He had just gotten back to work at a new job after being out of work for a time. He makes six bucks more an hour now. He is getting ahead. I felt really happy for him.

We scooched down and looked at the frame together in a male-bonding moment that defied our age difference. We marveled at the lack of scale rust and the corrosion-free frame of a truck from the southern United States.

He renewed his vows with the truck, and I could sense his true joy for finding something in such good condition.

I walked away to purchase the new battery in order to be able to mow the dandelions before the sun went down; he lit up a smoke and stood back from his truck to take it all in again.

It took three minutes. It was probably the best three minutes I had yesterday.

Oh, yeah, he is getting some new tires soon.

When I left the yard I was feeling a little grouchy about the condition of my old mower. Upon my return to the house, I installed the new battery and then mowed the lawn. I flicked on the mower's yellowing headlights as the sun dropped below the tree line. Suddenly, I was sure that I could make this mower last at least twenty more years.

Hardcovers, Easy Questions, and Silver Linings

While not much of a student, I have always been an eager learner. I love figuring things out. Directions can be referred to but only after I stare at the task at hand for a time.

I must admit that over the years I have experienced many moments of kicking myself after finding that the directions made some things far easier than the intensive staring and pondering. That comes before the crinkling and unfolding of multilingual descriptions typically provided in the package of recently purchased problematic devices and projects.

When I do know something that other people seem to have difficulty grasping, I enjoy offering a hand and then telling them that it took me forever to learn how to do it, as well. It's a good way to make a friend or two. People enjoy it when you tell them that you are just a bit dumber than they are.

We are all mopes in one way or another; there's no shame in that.

I feel my saving grace is that I was blessed with at least a modicum of common sense, a love of reading, and the ability to work my way through the problems that sometimes slow down my attempts to run near the back of the pack in the human race.

Some of this was learned while spending time with my dear grandfather. A life-long member of the fire service, John Coleman Miller was the fire chief in the city of Auburn, Maine, from 1950 to 1969.

He grew up in Manchester, New Hampshire, and came from a firefighting family. One of his uncles, in the early twentieth century, lost an eye fighting a bombastic conflagration in Manchester. Rather than retire, he took over manning one of the fire watch towers in that city. There's some irony in the fact that they put the one-eyed guy in charge of watching for fires, but it was a great story my grandfather shared with me.

Young John manipulated his way into the firehouse by taking care of the stable of work horses that served their life's purpose pulling fire apparatus throughout that industrial city. People tend to forget how important firefighting was around the turn of the century. In this day and age, with the advances in building codes, alarms, and mandatory sprinkler systems, the danger of losing an entire city block to a fire is far less likely.

John's second career was that of a Nazarene minister. Grampa was all about the fire and much less about the brimstone.

He was a kind and considerate man, polite, well-spoken, well-read, and much-loved by anyone who ever met him. He was also an extremely tough man. He had seen plenty of death, caused by smoke and fire, first-hand. Long before Scott oxygen packs and modern safety gear, he was running into burning buildings and hauling people out. He led through example, and he was treasured by those who followed him into the flames.

His incessant cough, which I can imitate perfectly after hearing it for my entire life, was caused by the steady influx of smoke inhaled doing what he loved the most. I don't remember a conversation with him where I did not hear three rhythmic, hacking coughing attempts to clear out the un-clearable. It was a signature wake-up sound in his home, and while probably painful and annoying, he never once mentioned that it bothered him. It signified to me that he was there, somewhere in the house.

It's funny how one person's life-long malady increased another person's comfort level, but that's what his coughing did for me.

One of my favorite photographs of him has been shared a couple of times in my social media pursuits. I collected it from an old Lewiston *Sun Journal* article. In the black-and-white photo, the chief's face is covered with soot, obvious sadness, and despair as he takes a break from rescue breathing into the mouth of one of his now-deceased officers. He had dragged the man out of the burning building during a late-night blaze. I still look at it, and I can almost feel his anger at the loss of a man, a firefighter, and a friend.

In his retirement, when I spent time at his home, he was always willing to grab a book off one of the higher shelves of his library of well-worn hardcovers. I would just need to point it out, and he would reach up and grab several books for me to choose from. I was always welcome to look through the lower shelves, but the books needed to be returned to their slots on the varnished pine shelves.

His television was not turned on for entertainment purposes. We were always welcome to listen to the radio, read whatever and as much as we wanted, play checkers and other games, or go out and wander around in the woods surrounding his retirement home on a small mountain in Raymond, Maine. *The Today Show* and *NBC Nightly News* were staples and a time for us to be silent and well-behaved. He relished information.

My grandfather valued common sense, questions, and learning though doing. I never heard him brag, but he could answer just about any question about almost any topic.

When I asked him about World War II, he presented me with a dog-eared copy of *Thirty Seconds over Tokyo* by Captain Ted W. Lawson. He advised me that it would be a good book to read. It was. I was nine years old, and he quizzed me on some of the details during a rainy Friday afternoon.

When I was able to tell him the name of the plane that Lawson piloted, the *Ruptured Duck*, he made me a maple-syrup-and-vanilla-ice-cream sundae. He always added whole walnuts. The jar of bright red maraschino cherries was pulled from the refrigerator as if life could not go on without one for the sundae and a spare, or two, to pop into his mouth. He made a goofy face and crossed his bright blue eyes like Jerry Lewis would. We laughed, and then we ate the sundaes.

One afternoon, when I asked him what was meant by the term "BTU" or "British Thermal Unit," my inquisitive nature led me to an afternoon of study regarding the subject. He handed me a stack of old, loosely bound books he had saved from his days of studying all there was to know about fire.

A few questions followed. I don't remember all of them, but I got one of them wrong. He advised me to review the information again. I did. When he later inquired about the topic, he didn't change the question in order to make me feel foolish; he asked me the exact question that I had missed, probably out of his natural sense of fairness. I have never found need to regurgitate that information again, but I do recall that it was a question about the temperature at which water has its greatest density.

It's thirty-nine degrees Fahrenheit, by the way.

He knew how to keep me busy, and would entice me to learn more by offering me a few shots with an ancient, Allen and Wheelock, .22-caliber revolver. The irony in this was that, after a stern safety lesson in the proper handling of the tiny old firearm, we took turns shooting at wooden matches stuck into the top of a weather-cracked gray cedar fence post in the woods behind his home.

Gramps was always finding a way to share lessons in fire and firearm safety.

Our goal was to light the matches by skimming the projectiles over the tips of the strike-anywhere fire sticks. He was a remarkable shot and could light them up with much regularity. I got the hang of it, and I lit off a few. A small pail of water was kept close by for dousing the flames if, for some reason, the wind did not snuff out the flare-ups.

We counted the matches when we were done, and after making sure we had picked all of them up, he directed me to toss them into the pail of water—one last safety measure.

As we walked through the high summer grass, perfect for picking and chewing in the corner of your mouth, he told me that my mother was a good shot as a little girl and that she had lit some matches with the same pistol—a short history lesson as we wandered uphill to put things away and discard the burned out matches and soot-stained water from the dented galvanized pail.

One glorious fall day in the early 1980s, Gramps showed up at our house just south of Bangor. He had brought me his old Marlin Model 336 .30-30 hunting rifle. He'd determined that since I was beyond the age of eighteen and had taken up outdoor pursuits, I would be better off with the rifle than he was. It was well-worn but had a lovely patina from years of being carried much but shot little. I don't believe my grandfather ever fired at an animal, but he loved being in the woods, and taking a gun for a walk was more of a traditional thing for him.

That very winter, our home out on Route 9 burned to the ground while all of us were away. It was January. The fire department came, but the water pumps on at least one of the trucks became frozen and inoperable. It made no difference as the old place, formerly a general store, was too far gone to be saved by anyone.

As you can imagine, everything was lost as the place collapsed into the stone-and-mortar walled basement. All items returned to the earth in more or less the same form as they had begun; that is, as ash and dust.

The old Marlin was only one of many items that were never recovered. We lost my young dog, Gonzo, as well. He succumbed to the smoke. His body was retrieved by one of the firefighters before it was consumed by the flames that could not have been fought with any hope of success. I don't know why that makes me feel better about it, but it does.

My dad later buried Gonzo up in the woods behind where the old house once stood.

John Miller, of course, came up from southern Maine immediately to aid the family and kick through the ashes, as was his former professional proclivity. He spoke to the firefighters and local chief about the cause. It was never able to be determined, but the wood stove was suspect.

He used a metal detector in the area where I had stored the old rifle. Looking through the ashes and cinder below the area where my closet once was, he discovered a ball of melted sterling silver that had once been the twelve settings of silverware he and my grandmother had purchased as a wedding gift for my mother and father. The dark-stained walnut presentation case was long gone, of course.

John Miller found no sign of the steel remnants of the rifle. He was sad and offered to purchase another rifle for me. I declined; it would never have been the same.

He passed away, late at night, in the early 1990s. He spent his last days weakened by congestive heart failure, coughing repeatedly, but he managed to tell some fantastic jokes. We knew it was time, and he did, too.

The notification of his death came to me in error. I had just taken an arrestee to the Penobscot County Jail when, sometime around midnight, my dispatcher radioed that I needed to respond to a home where an elderly man had just passed away. I called into dispatch for the address, and he, without any knowledge of my grandfather's name or condition, said, "It's John Coleman Miller." He then gave my mom and dad's address. I left work immediately to be with my family.

In the end, I felt that he would have enjoyed knowing that his last call for service was broadcast by a police and fire dispatcher. He lived with those voices hailing over the gray speakers of various Motorola two-way radios for most of his adult life. It only made sense that the voices would announce his passing.

We still have that ball of silver. It's rough, misshapen, and black with soot from that cold night. It's in a cardboard box at my parent's place. We talked about having it melted into something meaningful for them, but it already was something meaningful, and you shouldn't try to re-form a memory, whether good or bad.

I think that soot-covered ball of silver represents my grandfather quite well.

The Best That He Has

His clothes were not new, and they probably belonged to several other people prior to ending up on his back. You could see, as we passed him from time to time, that he only had one outfit—dirty tan pants, some kind of shirt, and an old sports jacket that was far too big for him.

I never paid attention to his shoes.

The route to the church varied, but we occasionally drove past the man sitting on his stoop in front of an unpainted and weathered clapboard-sided building.

I came to realize, in later years, before the structures were torn down, that the paint had become bleached and dull from being pounded by snow and rain, later left naked to fade in the hot summer sun. There were spots where the former coating of paint had been more resilient, but those spots were few.

Still, it was the man I watched for. I don't ever remember seeing his face, but as a youngster, I pictured it covered with gray whiskers in need of a trim, similar to the way I look now, forty-five years later, when I skip the razor on days off in the summer. If I were to describe it, I might say rough, old, and unkempt.

I rode to and from the church with the pastor. On Sunday mornings in the late fall and winter, we went in early to turn up the heat and bring the concrete block structure up to an adequate temperature for the elderly ladies who would soon inhabit the forward pews. I call it "adequate" because that is all it was. It never seemed warm to me. It was made clear that heating the building was an expense that needed to be reined in.

The elderly ladies usually wore their dark blue or gray full-length wool coats through most of the service. The pastor sometimes got an earful from them regarding how chilly it was inside.

In the summer, I would catch a ride to church well before services started. We would turn on box fans and open the windows to freshen up the old place. During the downtime, I might even return wayward hymnals and hard-covered bibles to their proper storage slots on the back of the pews.

Sometimes, on the drive home from church, depending on our route, we'd roll by the stoop where the man sat. I don't recall ever seeing any children, but I am sure there were some, and I assume they wore similar clothing.

It was on one of those trips when I asked the pastor why the man was always wearing the same tattered tan pants and improperly sized sports coat. I don't think I verbalized it in the same manner that I wrote that sentence, but he understood my question.

He was no stranger to growing up with little. He shared stories of a post-war family led by a widowed mother who toiled away doing shift-work at the paper mill in his hometown. He had four brothers and one sister. His father had been killed in the prime of his life while working in the woods in western Maine; he had been a lumberman.

Adversity to him was as normal as a warm bed, clean clothes, and plenty to eat was to me, the observant and inquisitive boy in the back seat.

I believe the most profound words in our lives are sometimes missed because we are too busy waiting for an opportunity to be profound ourselves. When you are nine or ten years old, being profound is not even on the agenda.

It is doubtful that the minister knows that what he said became an internalized firewall for me. Over the years, it helped me remain silent when I found myself being judgmental about how someone appeared, how they were dressed, whether they were fat, skinny, poor, or showed up dressed in someone else's old and ill-fitting clothes.

I think his stories about growing up in a hardscrabble way had an effect on me. I learned that someone's outward appearance has nothing to do with their heart or intentions, but it also gave me the ability to hit pause before I judged someone.

I don't write this to tell you that I have never partaken in the evil human sport of making fun of someone, because I have. I am as guilty as anyone else who's joining judgmental conversations.

His eight words are a simple reminder for me that we never know exactly what kind of terrain another person has had to travel to get to their current place in life.

The pastor's words were clear, "Son, maybe it's the best that he has."

That pastor was my dad, and I can assure you that those eight words were among the best gifts he ever gave me.

Kind Breezes, Naval Jelly, and a Perfect Summer Day

It was a perfect summer day—not the kind of perfect when you do all the right things, or get a lot done, but because it reminded me of a summer day in my youth.

This was the kind of day that I tell people about when they ask about summer in Maine.

Seventy-three degrees, cloudless sky, low humidity, and a slight breeze that somehow pushes me back on to a Little League field in Bridgton, Maine.

I am behind home plate with a hand-me-down catcher's mitt and a mask with straps that have been stretched out by better catchers with bigger heads.

I am but a poseur in another man's armor.

I adjust it one more time before Robbie throws a pitch resembling a strike. I generally sucked as a catcher—oh, and as a hitter—but I could catch most of those pitches that resembled a strike.

I remembered that today. I don't have any idea why. The more I move forward in life, the further my mind takes me back.

I had no glorious moments on the field. Truth be told, I enjoyed Little League because, from time to time, we were allowed to ride bicycles to the field from our home on the Ridge Road.

These rides were the greatest. Freedom in front of me as I piloted my red Western Flyer from behind the chrome handlebars. I so clearly recall the small freckles of rust that developed on those bars because of the improper storage techniques employed by the owner.

My dad got me my own jar of naval jelly at the Western Auto. I applied it liberally, rinsing with painfully cold well water gushing from a green garden hose.

I had my own SOS pad, given to me by my mother, but only when it became too worn for cleaning the pots and pans in the country kitchen of the old brown farmhouse with a rusty metal roof.

The plethora of cable-connected lightning rods pointed at the sky and defied it to strike again as the storms boiled up and out of the Mount Washington Valley.

I kept the SOS pad under the back porch for moments when the rusty-freckling became too much for the naval jelly to handle. I also stored a quarter can of all-purpose Singer sewing machine oil under that porch. I used that on the chain and anything else that seemed to thirst for lubrication.

I wonder if that can is still there, rotting away in the dirt and duff of forty-five years of fallen maple leaves and other assorted wind-blown lawn dander.

It was that kind of summer day—the kind of summer day we wait for all year. We are elated when it arrives, but more so because of the places we allow the breeze to carry us.

We wonder about a can that is surely rusted and gone, but our true wondering moments are about how many more summer days we will be able to recollect those simple pleasures that cost so little and mean so much.

Like the oil can, our true hope is that we will someday ride into someone's memory like the breeze of a perfect summer day. We can simply hope that they think fondly of us, resting under years of fallen maple leaves and other assorted wind-blown lawn dander.

I hope your day was half as good as mine.

The Bus Driver

The day I became a fan of the manual transmission is seared into my brain. Oddly, every time I pass a dairy farm, no matter where I travel, I get an odiferous flashback to a manual-shifting Bluebird bus, built on an International chassis.

You would think my first day of school would bring back other memories. I guess it does, but feeling abandoned by your mother and being thrown into a roving wagon full of runny noses and brand-new sneakers just aren't what I wanted to get at today.

I do remember crying and hoping that the tears would be invisible to the other kids heading to Ms. Gilmore's half-day kindergarten class. Thinking back to that September day in 1968, I know that the others didn't notice my sadness due to the fact that they had just gone through the same thing. We were all in this mess together.

Thank God for Richard, our standard transmission-shifting, dairy-farming driver. He smiled a little as I boarded the bus. It was the smile of a man who had been up for a while. Little did I know that driving the school bus full of miniature ruffians was probably the easiest part of his day. His green work shirt matched his green work pants; both faded to a different hue, a uniform of sorts. It was the uniform of a man who could drive stick. I noted the dog-legged lever topped with a faded-black shift knob. Inscribed into the top of that knob was a white outlined schematic, placed there to aid in smooth shifting travel down Route 302.

The motion of the initial launch, or lurch, caused the students to collectively rock back and then forth in the green vinyl seats. As velocity was gained, the shifts became smoother. I watched Richard masterfully upshift and downshift all the way to the schoolhouse. The squeaking clutch spring was the indicator that downshifting had begun, and that meant the addition of another person you hoped would not notice that there was space in your seat. I never wanted a window. Aisle seats on buses—and on airplanes later in my life—are always preferable for those of us who like to observe things.

As the year rolled on and cooler weather caused the heater fans to drown out the sound of the engine, I noted that the smell of Holsteins and their various leavings often permeated the cabin of the Bluebird. I recognized the smell of cows, and, by that point, it was clear to me that Richard was a dairy farmer both before he picked us up and probably long after he dropped us off. Richard rarely talked. He was a focused pilot. Double clutching from time to time, I watched him row through the gears and dreamed of the day that I could drive a truck, bus, or anything with that magical lever on the floor. Thoughts of fast cars and motorcycles would come much later.

Sometimes on the way to the grocery store, our family Ford would pass Richard's farm. The bus in those days would be parked at his house. It was a white clapboard-covered farmhouse with crooked additions; one big barn full of bovines. Old farm equipment and tractors were parked in various places. The air was thick with Richard's cologne.

During the daily bus rides, I mimicked his moves when I knew no one was watching: left foot pressing the invisible clutch, right hand shifting the same pattern that Richard did. I didn't even mind the smell of the cows. It was a reminder that Richard was in control. I don't ever remember grinding a gear. I was smooth.

I never really wanted the green Dickies shirt and pants set. It was cool on Richard, but I knew I would never be able to pull off that look.

Later in life, in the driver's seat of my buddy's '76 Ford F-250, I learned the dark art of double clutching. I also learned that gas wasn't cheap but worth every penny. I really was quite happy just riding around. I still am.

With the 460 V-8 "camper special" option under the hood, the ten-ply tires took a beating at stop lights. Believing that the ladies wanted to see black smoke was only a bonus byproduct of the visceral pleasure that dumping the clutch brought to our sixteen-year-old souls. U-joints feared us.

Driving home after a double feature at the drive-in movies, we had the windows down to clear out the smoke of Swisher Sweets. My hand rested on the faded black shift knob. I could feel the slightly raised schematic pattern under my palm. As we passed a small dairy farm, I smelled Richard's cologne and, just for a minute, I was driving a school bus down Route 302. Hopefully no one would notice that I wasn't wearing green Dickies.

Look at the Mantel

Stumbling through my life has been interesting. I think I appear well put together, possibly normal to some. My path has never been well planned, and I am in no way complaining. I am jealous of those who have a firm grasp on where they are going.

As a poor planner, I might get lost in a conversation with someone and yet never learn their name. I get engrossed in the mundane because somewhere in the mundane I find importance.

I watch people's eyes and the corners of their mouth when I meet them. Those are two places where a story begins, and I am a sucker for a good story. I don't want to hear one that ends perfectly, because I know mine doesn't. I spent many a road trip with my great friend Paul discussing the things that we enjoyed the most in life. We both agreed that the best experiences in life were fraught with some tragedy, failure, and a little luck.

None of the lessons I value have come from a book or classroom. Sure, those are the places where you should be made hungry to know more; places to develop a thirst for a few more quenching drops of clarity.

Most of what you need to know about a person is sitting right in front of you. Throughout my career, whenever I enter a home, I look at the mantel in the living room. The bookshelves and refrigerator hold many clues, as well. The things a person places on their mantel are important to them.

Family photos, vacation pictures, diplomas, certificates indicating the completion of a program of sobriety, wedding pictures, model cars, crosses, and trophies indicating a third-place finish. Some homes don't have a mantel, so a person who is inquisitive needs to look around at about eye level to see the things that are valued. It might be a prominent tattoo, a letter from their father, a locket from their mother. You can find it; you just need to take the time to look for it.

When you look at a friend's photo on Facebook, look into the background. You will find the things that are important to them—their children, a rosary, a puzzle, silver candlestick holders, or an empty chair.

The point? Don't always focus on the new hairstyle, glasses, or clothing. Look deeper to know more about them and converse about it when you see them. There is far more to a person than how they look, or even what they write as a status.

Look for their mantel, and you will be a better friend.

Paying Attention

I think paying attention to those around us is the most under-utilized ability we possess.

I liken it to the saxophone solo in the middle of the Hall and Oates classic, "She's Gone." You are probably too busy with your riffs, runs, and embellishments as you sing it out loud in your car to even notice the good work being done by the woodwind section. Listen to it the next time it comes on; you'll be surprised that you never noticed it before.

I walked through our lobby the other day and saw a homeless man picking up some of his belongings, which we had secured for him after he had been arrested. If you are reading this on an electronic device, or on paper, I guarantee you have more to your name than this man did.

One of the bags contained two five-cent returnable cans. They were important to him. You and I might kick them out of the way while we walk down the sidewalk. Ten cents was important to him. Sure, he would pick up more as he wandered, but these were his security, his investment, his savings.

I asked him how he was doing and he smiled and said he was better now that he was out of jail. I concurred that jail sucks. I told him to have a good weekend and hit the "3" on the elevator.

As I rode upward with my $2.24 hot coffee, I "noticed" him. Sure, I had made conversation, but it took me about thirty seconds to realize his situation, to realize the sour odor was his, to realize how I had spoken to him kindly but was truly dismissive. He was going to have a crappy weekend.

I felt like a jerk.

I got to the third floor and hit the down button. I dug through my pocket to see how much cash I had left, not because I wanted to pay penance for my dismissiveness but maybe to make a few minutes of his day better.

He was still there when I arrived. I told him that I wanted him to get something good to eat and tried to slip him what I could. He would not take it because he said he'd recently gotten some disability money. I asked him how much, and he said he had about $400 for the month. I was able to get him to take enough for dinner and then exchanged a few more words before he loaded up his bags and headed out.

Why the story? To point out that we pass by people every day, and we fail to notice them. Sometimes you can't help them out financially, but you can try to be a little kinder, a little less dismissive. I fail at this all the time.

I write this only as a reminder to myself that I should try to do better.

The Librarian

I never knew her name, but she treated me kindly. That's what I remember most about her.

I was lucky enough to grow up in a time when new sneakers came once a year, information was gleaned through the use of someone else's encyclopedias, and television was something you did for half an hour or so after supper—possibly an hour if we kept the volume down so mom could forget we were in the living room.

Baths were on Saturday night. My mom would throw a drop of Clorox in the tub. I was always darn clean and fresh-smelling for Sunday school, I can tell you that.

What in the world did we do to make the days pass? We walked to school, made forts, got into fist fights with our best friends, and no one called the cops. No one had a cellular phone to call the cops, and we sure weren't going to tell our parents that we'd gotten in a tussle with our pal. That was kept a secret because we knew we could work it out within a day or so.

I also went to the library.

Between the third and sixth grade, I was in the tiny local library at least twice a week. It was about a block from my house, and, if I cut through the backyards and around the broken fence, I could be there in less than five minutes. I cut through many backyards; no one even cared. I was cautious to stay on the worn footpaths—even trespassing was a polite endeavor.

The granite library had huge multi-paned windows that allowed you to see stacks and stacks of faded-yellow *National Geographic* magazines as you walked up the steps. The dark wooden door opened unusually easy for me.

The craftsman that hung that door probably knew that it was important for it to swing easily. It needed to be used. I think he thought of that when he checked it one last time; he probably said, "Perfect," just before packing up his tools.

The librarian said very little, but she always smiled. I remember learning the Dewey Decimal System from my third-grade teacher, Mrs. Guptill. I was so excited to be able to peruse the card catalog with confidence when I felt I was being watched by the librarian.

She was always helpful if a book was not where I believed it should be; she was willing to check the return box if there were books missing from the shelves, and she never acted too busy to help.

I checked out the maximum number of books and tore through them like they were going to be missing when I woke up the next morning. I always finished them within a week or so, and I was never late returning any books except the one about the United States Coast Guard. I misplaced it. I panicked. Would she let me back in? Would she make me pay a fine?

I had no money, especially for fines. Would there be jail time? Worst of all, I didn't want to disappoint her. That's the truth.

I found the book. I don't recall now where I found it, but I did. It was about a week late.

I had stayed clear of the library during the week of the missing book. I couldn't face her. I had placed the other books in the return box on a day when she was busy helping someone else.

I moved quickly. I was always quiet so there was no need to change my modus operandi—smooth, very smooth.

When the books hit the bottom of that wooden box, I thought for sure she would be able to tell that there were only three. In my mind, I felt that she would even know which book was missing by the lack of resonance in the drop. She never even looked up.

When I went back with the book about the Coast Guard, I had to come face to face with her. I knew that I could not get away with just dropping it in the box. It was time—time to look her in the eye. I needed to pay the fine, meet my maker.

I told her that it was late about the same time that she opened the book to check the red rubber-stamped date. I think my voice shook. She just smiled and told me that she was glad to have the book back and asked me what I was going to read next.

I was a free man—free to roam among the stacks and borrow any book that I wanted, free to pull out the long drawers of yellowing cards, free to sit at the huge slab-like tables and thumb through *National Geographic* magazines. What a great feeling it was.

Oddly, this brings me to my point. Over the thirty years of being a police officer, I often think of the grace that librarian offered me. In situations where we are able to use discretion in dealing with a problem, these tiny life lessons mold us.

If I could offer a break, I always have. I always will. When it is not possible, I sometimes feel bad. Yes, cops feel bad.

I never knew her name, but she treated me kindly. That's what I remember most about her.

Take your child to a library. Let them look through the books, select one, make them return it on time. Little lessons—they mold you.

Dan

One of the most oft-heard comments I get, no matter where my words find a place to sit, is "You're showing your age." It seems to happen when I share a song from the '70s, or the memory of a commercial or television show from the '60s.

I know that it's an off-the-cuff remark made by folks who are, many times, just about the same age as I am. I relish the comment more as time goes by. Here's why.

I traveled through my life wanting to become older, seasoned, and well-informed. Upon my arrival at what I always thought would be a perfect season of life, carrying a fair amount of general knowledge, some common sense, and a truckload of experiences that others might have liked to have had, suddenly I am giving away what no one really wants after all.

When I was lucky enough to be able to afford a house in the '80s, it was already old. I have written about it. That house taught me more about life than any one specific thing I have ever experienced. I learned to thaw out frozen pipes; remove water from the basement; replace windows, floors, toilets, leaking pipes, and both seal up the flashing on chimneys and clean out the caked creosote within.

And do you know what I did when I didn't have any clue what do next? I walked across the street to see Dan Pelletier.

He was in his seventies, owned every tool that would fit on a perfectly laid out pegboard, and provided me just as much sarcasm about my lack of marketable skills as information to help me do the job—a perfect blend of sweet and sour.

I would return to the house to work on whatever tragedy had befallen me, and, in an appropriate amount of time—either minutes or hours—he would saunter across the street with a pair of work gloves and a smirk. He always helped me finish the job.

One day, when I was particularly frustrated about a plumbing job I was working on down in the dirt-floor basement, I made the mistake of telling Dan I'd about had enough and was going to call a plumber. He knew I didn't have the money for a plumber.

Dan glared down at me while holding a flashlight and said words that echo through my skull to this day: "Are you telling me that you believe that any man is smarter or better than you are?"

This was not a slam on anyone in the plumbing trades. This was how Dan dumped a wheelbarrow load of self-confidence into a twenty-something-year-old kid. It felt like a kick in the ribs, but it was really a boot appropriately applied to a spot a little lower on my anatomy.

The pipes in and out of the water heater were repaired with some of the ugliest solder joints ever applied to copper. No leaks appeared. No plumber was called.

It went like that for a lot of years, and a lot of jobs.

Dan revealed his age to me every time we talked, and I never once thought that was a bad thing. If you tell me I am showing my age, I'll take it as a compliment.

When Did "Mad" Become the New Normal?

Please don't turn this into commentary on the political climate, because I reject it. It has been going on far longer than this last election cycle. I just can't seem to pin down the time frame.

It seems like the emotion that gets the most "likes" on a Facebook feed is plain, old, angry.

There are hundreds of emojis for this. Even the Snoopy emoji has an angry mode. I don't remember Snoopy ever being mad about anything except the Red Baron. This I understood, as Snoopy had his dog house shot to pieces. There is room for anger when your home has been "Swiss-cheesed" in a fly-by shooting. Snoopy never posted it on his newsfeed. He fixed up the dog-house and returned to napping mode.

If a beagle can do it, we can too.

A tirade against the other driver who wronged you, a shocking and curse-filled rant against a store clerk who overcharged you, a person who wouldn't move their grocery cart out of our way as we sped through the spice aisle. I don't know, but I personally have had enough.

See, my last paragraph ended with a similar tone. I withheld the expletives and threats of minor and unnecessary violence against them. There was just no need.

Maybe the things we used to say at home to relatives, best friends, or annoying acquaintances have just bubbled to the surface because of our ability to air them to the world—aka our friend's list, Twitter feed, or Instagram account.

It's kind of sad.

In December of 2016, I was flying to Florida and ended up getting into LaGuardia a little late. I barely made my connecting flight, and, when I did sit down, I found myself by a pleasant woman with a journal. She wrote all the way to Florida. I was amused by it all. She quietly wrote in beautiful cursive, and oddly, it made me feel comfortable—just a smooth cadence with a very nice pen. She seemed happy. Every now and then I would watch her put the pen to her bottom lip and look out at the clouds. Each time, she appeared to have a minor epiphany that I could sense by the way she moved and returned to writing the beautiful script. It was calming.

Across the aisle were six passengers, two rows of three each. Three women, three men. They were together. They were loud. What struck me is that they seemed to enjoy cutting down just about anyone who walked by. They were mean people.

I cannot tell you that I have never said mean things, but I always feel bad afterward. I have a really good mother. She rides with me every day in the back of my mind. Sometimes she shuts my mouth with a whisper in my ear. She doesn't know it, but it's true. "Timothy!" That's really all she needs to say to me.

Suddenly, my lifetime skill set of listening to group discussions around me took over. I heard them talking about wanting to see the state of Maine. It felt like they might start saying nicer things, and I put my head back to nap before takeoff.

I was wrong.

The loudest and most annoying member of the group said something that made me contemplate becoming a loud Mainer. He said he would like to go to Maine but did not want to deal with the overwhelmingly "toothless population." My eyes opened, but my head stayed pinned against the rich Corinthian-leather headrest. I tuned my left ear to the conversation like a Maine whitetail hearing a snapping branch in mid-November.

They all laughed. It could have been funny in the right venue, but it struck me differently. I felt it was a little mean. I know some other passengers from Maine had boarded the plane with me and that one of them was an older woman about three rows in front of me. It didn't appear that she had heard it.

I turned to make sure I could observe the face of the man who said it. His wife elbowed him and said, "Be careful, there might be some people from Maine on this flight." There was. He was smug, superior, and a few other "S" words. I held my tongue; maybe there would be an opportunity later. I said a little prayer. Yes, I do that. Don't be offended.

Upon landing in Tampa, the rush to get out of seats in order to stand up and block the aisle took place as planned. The man was up and out, grabbing his carry on from the overhead bin directly over my seat. I stood up abruptly and reached in to grab my own carry-on. We were together at last.

I tempered my words with a smile and told him that Mainers had been blessed with superior hearing since we had been short-changed in the dental department. He looked perplexed. I told him that his wife had been right. There were Mainers sitting nearby. His face dropped. He remembered the statement, and probably her elbow to his ribcage.

He said, "You heard that?" I said that I did. He said, "I'm so sorry." I told him that it was no problem. I didn't need to say anything else. His eyes told me that he wasn't mean at all. He was cracking a joke that I have heard many times. I wasn't mad any longer, and he wasn't mean any longer. I am far from perfect and have said some pretty stupid things. I don't need a lawyer to confront an issue, and I felt better. I think he did as well.

The woman with the journal continued to write. She was waiting patiently and still had plenty of pages to fill.

I look back on that flight and think that I should have talked to her more and listened to others less. Maybe we should all just get a journal and write pleasant things that others will never hear. This world might become a better place.

Just Inside the Barn Door

I sat just inside the open barn doors staring at the sunset with my long-time pal last week. He doesn't read my page, or the Bangor Police Department page. He refuses to open a Facebook account. I cannot say that I blame him.

He doesn't watch national news channels, but neither do I. I try to get my news through reading multiple and varied websites.

I read a couple of newspapers, but overall I just collect my news in snippets. I don't want to depend on anyone else to determine what it means. I can figure that out, and I am really not all that bright.

I take a little of that back. I do find myself watching the early, early morning national news broadcasts.

The big-three—or former big-three—networks have a junior varsity team that reports the news in the wee hours of the morning. Since I try to go through my emails sometime between 0400 and 0500 each day, I like to watch those folks out of the corner of my eye. They appear to be breaking into the national news game. Sometimes they look to be a little tired, and some of them are very good at what they do.

I like to watch anyone who is just starting out—rookies at the police department, kids who are just starting school, and teens who have just recently been assigned to work a cash register for the first time.

Yesterday, at an undisclosed location, I explained to one nice young lady that I had only asked for fifty dollars cash back, not one hundred and fifty dollars.

She was happy I gave the money back—seemed surprised, actually.

That's sad in itself.

She was embarrassed that I had to count it back to her, but I think she learned something. And I told her I had done much worse things back in the day when I ran a cash register for the first time. Her flushed cheeks would soon clear up, but she wasn't short one hundred bucks at the end of her shift.

I later shared with my buddy, anecdotally, why I believe people read the flight of ideas that I present on Facebook. I told him that, even in the face of some negative days, I try to post positive things on the interweb. No, I don't always think, or do, positive things, but I told him that it helps me remain positive in my outlook.

I read to him a post that I had written about our time eating snow cones and watching his springer spaniels. He pondered it for a time and finally said that he understood. He believed that I'd captured the moment quite well.

As men, we rarely talk about capturing moments. We capture them, but we let chatter about the moments slide by. Maybe we feel embarrassed about feeling something at all.

We don't like to shed tears; we certainly don't like people to see us doing it. I find tears can cleanse more than your eyes, but I still try to hide them when I can.

We have emotional thoughts, but we don't want to be "that guy" who shares why it was emotional. I gave that up.

Some of my friends who might read my stuff from time to time think that I say too much—especially when I tell of my own embarrassing moments. I let that go as well.

For the record, I stumble along just like everyone else. Don't believe, for even one second, that I have it all figured out. I am working on it, though. Writing about it is just but one step in the process—just as important is taking the time to watch the sun go down through the open barn doors.

4.

Got Warrants?

"Got Warrants?" is a feature of the semi-humorous and marginally famous Bangor Police Department Facebook page.

Growing up, I looked forward to reading the police blotter columns in local papers. This is my homage to the good old days. All the stories are true. I avoid names or identifying features. I write it in the manner that I write everything—poorly.

"Got Warrants?" is intended to be read out loud to your spouse or significant other. Reading it to your kids at bedtime is fine by me. We keep it clean, but we keep it real.

Please avoid reading it to people who do not want to hear it. You know what I am talking about. They listen but do not laugh. They avoid eye contact and try to act like they are busy with something important, yet you read on. The fact that you don't even know them, and you are in a public restroom does make it a little weird. Do not be that person.

If "Got Warrants?" were an Axe body-spray fragrance, it would smell like cold coffee in a paper cup, intertwined with just a hint of Brut Classic cologne. You might catch a light whiff of leather polish in the air and, of course, Juicy Fruit gum. That stuff is awesome. Swoon, if you must.

* * *

Utilizing an aluminum pan to make an egg is something the officers of the Bangor Police Department fully understand.

Creating an egg on top of your roommate's head by using the pan as a weapon is never acceptable.

A man, who was sleeping on the couch, immediately rose to his feet when the pan struck his skull. The ringing in his ears was followed by a similar ringing sound in our dispatch center.

We are glad he called. We do not support the use of aluminum cookware in physical confrontations. The roommate admitted to holding some pent-up animosity from an argument that had occurred earlier in the day.

Charges were filed against the roommate. No hospitalization was necessary. Let us suggest a pillow or other soft item be kept handy for those moments when animosity is turned into physical force.

* * *

A cigar shop on Main Street welcomed the female patron but soon found out the humidor was not big enough for her poor behavior and rude manners. She was drunk, so let's not blame tobacco products. She refused to leave the intentionally smoky room. Cops were called. Officers arrived.

The lady did not listen to the kind words that were intended to move her along. She said things like, "What are you going to do, F@*!ing arrest me?" She also used other phrases that would lead you to believe that this is not a children's bedtime parable.

Incomplete and colorful phrases are the tools of those who have overindulged. Words can hurt, but they can also make you laugh.

We are highly trained to snicker internally. It helps on certain days.

We asked her to stop blocking the doorway and ease on down the road, or she would go to jail. She said, "Take me to jail, $@%k-it. If you don't, I am going to buy liquor and go drink it in the woods!" Threats like this can be hurtful, but we take in-service police academy training each year so that we can deal with the traumatic effects of D.S.S. (Dumb Statement Syndrome).

She was warned again. She still refused. She was arrested and continued to be angry and extremely vocal for our in-car studio monitors. She told officers that Osama bin Laden was still alive and that freedom is not free. Our cop knew the latter to be true but disagreed about OBL.

He stays informed by watching multiple news channels and is a slave to no single news source. It mattered not. She was dropped off at the jail and charged with disorderly conduct. These times do try us.

*   *   *

Officers were called to investigate the report of public indecency on the lawn of the library. This suspect was no-book worm, as he didn't have a library card. The complainant told the officer that she saw the man relieving himself while unabashedly flashing his naughty bits for the entire world to see.

One of our sergeants happened to be patrolling the downtown region and located the suspect at Pierce Park. The man was found hanging around near the statues of the log drivers who once roamed about on the huge timbers floated down our mighty Penobscot River.

The officer then went to the historic statuary and found the man. He was from Pennsylvania. The man had been drinking excessively. This necessitated his decision to uncover what should have been covered. The man was summoned for indecent conduct and given a one year criminal trespass warning for that area of the city. We now officially have no friends in Pennsylvania.

* * *

A man in Second Street Park made the decision to present his private parts in a manner that was not consistent with the appropriate way to introduce yourself to passers-by. A woman who had no choice but to look did not appreciate his gleeful response to the burning she felt in her retinas. Her pleas for him to stop did nothing to slow his somewhat offensive way of tanning his nether regions.

The sergeant located the suspect a short time later. The fluorescent orange shirt the suspect was wearing at the time of the incident was like a lighthouse to a weary sailor. Our sergeants like to be compared to sailors in many situations.

A conversation ensued, but the customary handshake was avoided. With the skill of a highly trained investigator, the sarge was able to elicit a confession about the illicit behavior. The man said, and I quote, "You caught me red-handed."

Controlling his urge to discuss the verbiage and all the connotations that were conjured up in his mind, the sergeant issued the man a summons for indecent conduct. The man signed the summons and will appear in court later this summer.

The man was told to keep the pen as a parting gift.

* * *

We received and responded to a report of a man who appeared to be wrapped in a clear, plastic trash bag. We found him in the center of Second Street Park.

This was odd, even to us.

The responding officers had no trouble seeing who they were dealing with as the caller had been correct in reporting that he was wrapped in clear plastic.

They spoke to the man, and positively identified him from previous dealings. They then confirmed that the man was wanted on active arrest warrants.

They took him into custody and unwrapped him prior to delivery to jail staff members.

*　　*　　*

After being called to a car burglary in progress, Bangor cops located a suspect in a nearby park. The suspect, wearing clothing similar to the man last seen rummaging through someone else's car, used a technique that never gets old—lying.

The subtle movement of the lips is one indicator that lies are being told, but is not the most reliable.

When the proceeds from the theft are recovered in one pocket, and medicinal, calming herbs (weed) are found in the other, always go with the "These are not my pants," defense.

No, I am not kidding. He told the officer that the pants belonged to a friend.

As our cop counted out the contents of the pockets, other officers aided in the investigation to find out which cars from the neighborhood were missing items.

The copious amount of coinage recovered from the "other guy's pants" seemed excessive. The suspect, who said his name was Joshua (always go with a biblical character's name first), told us that he had recently purchased a soft drink from a local bodega. He said he received the coins as change from the transaction.

Cops felt that the gold collectible coin, emblazoned with

Ronald Reagan's name, would not typically come back as change from a convenience store. "Joshua" said that the coin was a family heirloom that had been passed down for generations.

We wondered why the family heirloom had been discovered in the pocket of someone else's trousers. Apparently these pants, and this heirloom, "got around."

After further questioning, the man was found to be named Justin. Justin had bail conditions from previous interactions with law enforcement. Justin said he tried to tell the officers his real name earlier, but they would not listen—probably because they were still trying to process why the pants fit him so perfectly. Our guys and gals know that when they borrow other people's pants, the legs are always too long.

Justin was charged with burglary of a motor vehicle, theft, and violation of bail conditions. He swore that he had seen the individuals the officers had been looking for. He said he heard them running in the other direction while he wandered in the park. Of course you did, Justin. Of course you did.

* * *

The observant but drowsy officer wanted a coffee. As he sat at the drive-up window awaiting the sugar-and-cream-infused concoction, he peered through the glass at the vibrant and busy employees of America's #1 fast-food franchise.

As we all do, he was wondering if the pot of coffee was fresh. He was suspicious that he might be getting the final remnants of the formerly hot and glorious rejuvenating fluid. He also was observing a man who was ordering a sandwich at the counter. The cop recognized the man and knew for a fact that the man had a court-ordered curfew.

Unlike mom's curfews, these do not come with a verbal warning that your father will soon find out about the violation. Would our officer deny himself the first sip in order to do his duty?

The cavalier cop dismounted the Ford Interceptor and entered the late-night mecca of all that is fried and sesame-seed laden.

The man, who was about three hours overdue at his residence, suddenly recalled that he should have been home several hours ago (go ahead, face-palm). He then asked his new partner in late-night snacking if he could eat before going to jail. Our officer determined that a kinship had developed in that very short time.

This is where I would add Richard Marx soundtracks. I think of "Hold on to the Nights" as the theme song if this incident were to be put to music.

You can do that in your head. You're welcome.

After the chicken sandwich was gone and salt granules were scattered like the memory of the fries that once existed, the officer and the man traveled to jail together. Their bond was golden; like the arches that had brought them together in the first place.

*　　*　　*

The gentleman's club was not open yet, and the manager turned away three curious young men who wanted to be entertained. As the men left, one member of the trio—sporting tan pants—used a can of spray paint on the front wall.

Pent-up frustration manifests itself in many different ways. Apparently the ladies at the club are not the only ones being observed, and the "Rembrandt of Rustoleum" was caught on tape.

Cleverly, he painted a large "Z" on the outside wall. Was he Zorro? Had he come to help the poor girls that lived in the village of Dance Sans Blousia? Nope. Zorro never rocked the khakis, nor did he damage other people's property for no reason.

A short time later, the "Lords of the No-Lap-Dance" were

discovered walking up Main Street. Our officer recalled the clear photo of khaki-boy and his excellent paintsmanship. The man was charged with criminal mischief.

It is unclear if the squadron of testosterone-laden lads returned to the club to apologize or make their cash disappear into the recesses of questionable circumstances.

TC's Maxim #11: Placing portraits of presidents into panties is never the best use of your piggy bank's proceeds

* * *

Throwing your key card at the hotel clerk will not win you bonus points for future stays. Yelling that you want the clerk to do things to himself that would require a miracle of medical science to accomplish does not get you free drinks at the bar.

Still, the clerk pressed on and told the man that he needed to move his car out of a restricted parking area. After the outburst, the clerk asked Bangor's finest to tell the man it was time to move on.

Officers found him outside, inside of his car. When they spoke, the officers noted the strong odor of alcoholic refreshments. When asked how much he'd had to drink, the man said, and I quote, "A lot."

He told the cops that he was not driving the car but only "moving it" out of a space as requested by the pleasant clerk.

After the man exited the vehicle he told them that he was becoming a little "p#$$@d off." He then grabbed one of our cop's arms and screamed a little louder.

On his way to jail, the man was quieter. He was charged with OUI and was criminally trespassed from his accommodations. A bed was provided at another local B&B where crisp bacon was not served the following morning.

* * *

Bangor officers were called to a Sanford Street address to speak to two individuals who were screaming at one another. These same two people had been warned earlier by another officer. They were told if the police had to come back to squelch the noise, they would be going to jail.

This was the kind of loud that makes your hair hurt. This is not allowed by statute or by any civilized standards.

Both made claims that they had been assaulted by the other. There was no evidence of this. Solomon's wisdom was hoped for and then dispensed when the cops took both of them to jail.

In an effort to get in one last word, the woman told jail guards that the man was hiding meth in his underwear.

After a thorough strip search, it was determined that the lady was lying, but we felt she had won that round.

Forcing an unnecessary probe of your loved one's nether regions could be considered a win.

Touché ma'am. Touché.

* * *

The call came into our dispatch center as "suspicious." The caller said "a white male wearing a black sweatshirt was standing in front of the old YMCA staring at the flowers." The officers arrived to find exactly what the caller previously described. They did not find it suspicious at all.

In a world where we all have been cautioned to stop and smell the roses, why are we suspicious when someone actually follows through?

We always want you to call us; let's just not become too jaded.

*　　*　　*

A call of a family fight led our officer to a man standing outside his residence. While they stood there together, loud voices could be heard from within the house.

The officer observed an axe-handle that was leaning up against the wall. He then inquired about it and the man told him that he uses the tool handle as a cane. It is Maine. There are several axe handles in most every shed. The officer examined the axe handle and discovered that it had been customized with the rubber bumper from the bottom of a standard cane. Maine ingenuity level: Expert.

If Paul Bunyan had a limp, I believe he would have been proud to use the device.

The man told the cop that he was in the process of moving out when his fiancée threw a wooden lamp stand at his cat.

Our officer then entered the home and was verbally berated by the woman. She was easily heard. Oddly, she became louder as he got closer, but the change in pitch and volume did not increase because of the closure of space; it became louder by virtue of the woman's ability to ramp-up the noise level.

The officer was surprised that the cat had even stayed around long enough to become the intended victim of flying illumination devices.

The lady told the officer that the man had broken a piece of "art" that had originally belonged to her grandmother. The officer was informed that the axe-man had struck the woman with the handle, now posing as a cane.

The officer then returned to the porch and spoke to the axe-man, who admitted that he had broken a few things but had only struck the loud woman on the shoulder, just to get her attention. He added that he had only damaged his own personal property.

Based on the statements, the man was arrested and charged

with assault and a couple of counts of terrorizing as he had learned that the man slipped in a few death threats, as well. This was confirmed by independent witnesses.

The axe handle has been placed into the evidence locker. There are no patents currently pending on the design.

* * *

Hiding is an art, but most people do not practice it enough to become proficient. During a bail check on Fourth Street, Bangor officers discovered a man, intentionally covered in dirty laundry, under a desk. We do not need to be Kojak to do this job; believe me.

The man was found to have an active arrest warrant and was led outside to the waiting police cruiser. After a few more minutes, which included less seeking and some rather poor hiding, another man with an active warrant was discovered in the bathroom.

He was just standing there with the door shut. He really showed zero commitment to his craft. He was urine tested as his bail conditions allowed, and was found to have been using narcotics.

It was as if freedom had been sucked from the room by the loud, ceiling-mounted Honeywell ventilation fan. He was taken to jail. We think that people can do better.

* * *

During a recent traffic stop, one of our officers introduced himself to the occupants of a van that contained evidence of illegal drug activity. After the three occupants got out, one of them decided to leave, as he did not enjoy the company of the cop. I understand this. As the officer searched the car for further evidence, he found a sneaker sticking out from under a pile of clothing and dunnage in the back of the van. The sneaker contained a foot and the foot was attached to a man. The man had an active arrest warrant. The remaining two passengers did not recall how the man got there—completely normal reaction. But he still went to jail.

* * *

Is there a happier place on earth than Dunkin Donuts? We think not. That is why we are always a little confused when someone acts out in a way that causes their ejection from the grand gallery of glazed goodness. A man, whose last name is the exact opposite of "bad," was not being good (see what I did there). He told the officer that he had just arrived back in town but that he was still banned from most locations for generally acting like a knave. When the patient police officer told him that he was no longer welcome at the pearly gates of pumpkin spice, the non-compliant man told the cop that he would not leave, and that would force the officer to place him under arrest him. That is exactly what the cop did.

* * *

Officers were sent to a motel on outer Hammond Street. This particular auberge is known for its simple name and the fact that the innkeepers always provide adequate illumination for late-comers.

Cops went there to take the report of a person breaking out the windows. This is not the type of tomfoolery that makes other in-dwellers feel relaxed when smoothing the sheets with their weary bones.

A simple trip to the ice machine can turn into a scene from *The Walking Drunk*. It's not currently on Netflix, but we certainly become unwilling players in the pilot episode most every weekend.

The officer, known for his interminable spirit and the kind

eyes of a loyal retriever, was given the following information: A trio of revelers had consumed alcoholic beverages together for a substantial amount of time. One male participant of the gathering was told that he should slow down his intake. This makes sense.

The suspect became displeased. The first thing he did was to convene a group of sober peers to review the decision to close down the tap. I'm kidding; I kid. The outcast went all kinds of crazy on the other male and tackled him on the loosely tucked sheets that draped over the disheveled bed of disappointment.

The remaining members of the trio, formerly known as enjoying themselves, escaped the room to summon help. That's when the suspect started taking names and smashing glass. Lashing out is sometimes a cry for help, and that's where Bangor cops come in.

The now-bleeding and still-inebriated suspect went to the lobby area where he broke another window. Handcrafted broken glass seems so much more "artsy." He then ran for the wood line, where he attempted to hide in that pitiful way that people hide when drunk; we refer to it as "very poorly."

He was arrested for the crime of criminal mischief and charged with at least one other issue. He was taken to the emergency room during his victory lap to jail. Glass is sharp. He was not.

*   *   *

A local man, known for his ability to turn violating his bail conditions into a professional occupation, was asked to leave a local donut emporium. He was intoxicated and belligerent. No, I do not think donuts and alcohol mix. I also do not know how it is possible to become belligerent around the world's most perfect food, but I digress.

The Bangor officer arrived and noted that, while America runs on Dunkin, this man had added several quarts of malt liquor. That is not a featured "flavor shot." Let us place another violation upon his well-rounded resume. You might even knock the font size back a couple of notches so that he can get all the information on one sheet of acid-free and archive-safe, resume paper. Future employers do not have time to thumb through mad stacks of arrest references.

The officer offered to give him a "Bangor Mulligan." No, it is not an Irish cocktail. For the suspect, it is similar to accepting a gift card from an uncle you never really liked after he finished off the turkey stuffing at your mom's house during Thanksgiving in 1986. You were at the kid's table. The mulligan benefits would have allowed the man to walk away and allow a quiet and dark-roasted peacefulness to envelop the area. The suspect refused the kindly brewed cup of goodness.

Our officer quickly switched to French-press mode and arrested the suspect. He continued to be a tad angry with the officer. While at the jail, the suspect was asked why he had been arrested. The man told corrections officers that he had been "illegally hunting turtles." We don't even know the statute for such an offense, but I left a message for the good folks at the Maine Warden Service. We will take it as a confession to a crime that we do not believe occurred. For the record, we like turtles. They are quiet and pleasant creatures. We crave that kind of friendship.

* * *

The man, who'd stuffed one half-gallon of Lord Calvert Blended Canadian whiskey down his pants, was easily spotted.

A bottle that big tends to chafe the naughty bits unless you walk with the natural gait of a bow-legged contortionist. While we do not encourage the theft of talcum powder, we do suggest the use of such a product to ensure a smooth exit from the liquor aisle.

Gold Bond would work, but the peppermint-like tingle would cause a smirk to manifest itself upon your poker face, leaving the loss prevention agent to wonder why the limping man is sporting such a satisfied grin. The story gets better.

The man claimed that he was only stealing the bottle to help a friend who was struggling financially. He said if he used his ATM card to pay for the item, his parents (who have access to his account data) would know that he was in Bangor, Maine, rather than Oxford. That is where he was supposed to be that day. When I say "Oxford," I am not talking about the institute of higher learning. I am referring to Oxford, Maine.

He was summoned for the theft and criminally trespassed from the retail establishment for a year.

*　　*　　*

The scent is described as Sultry. Glamorous. Confident. A local woman represented all three descriptors quite well as she fled the Rite Aid store with the latest scent offering from Nicki Minaj. Who among us does not want to "Rule their queendom with Minajesty?"

I am not gonna lie. I long for a sultry floral gourmand scent that reigns with "luscious fruits and luxurious fresh florals draped in creamy vanilla and pure musks." Kudos to the writer of the Minajesty advertisements for their creativity in describing the aroma of their product. I would never have come up with the words, "draped in creamy vanilla and pure musks" on my own.

All I ask is that you pay for it instead of breaking into a sweat-covered sprint as you leave the store on shank's mare.

We are fairly sure that even one of our faster officers would not have been able to catch her as she had shotgunned a container of Muscle Milk prior to the perfume-inspired jaunt to who-knows-where. Not surprisingly, she did not pay for the Muscle Milk either.

I picture the hastily placed bottle teetering back and forth like a bowling pin that had been scuffed by the last ball in a badly played string.

Who was she? Will we need to track her by the scent of her new-found acquisition? Oh, wait! She left her friend behind, and she told us who the suspect was. We have scheduled her for some alone time. We have prepared a summons. The officer will be in touch. He will be sporting Old Spice. Hide downwind. The sporty freshness should arrive just prior to his undeniable charm.

*   *   *

A man in a red coat was clearly intoxicated and sleeping on a Rutland Street porch. The porch was not his to sleep on, and the homeowner wisely contacted us to arrange different accommodations.

Our officer (a busy young lad) noted that the man smelled of spirits and staggered, as people sometimes do after drinking several too many. When the cop asked him where he was headed, the man said he would like a ride to his grandparents' home in Eagle Lake. Eagle lake is 155 miles to the north.

Ain't nobody got time for that.

The man's continuous and clangorous use of the f-bomb caused Rutland Street porch lights to kick on faster than the man's common sense could be activated.

He did not heed the clear and concise warnings to quiet down and the young officer had no choice but to change the venue by applying the stainless restraint devices that we seem to use far too often when a moral compass has been lubed—improperly—with alcohol.

✳   ✳   ✳

We applaud the use of fire extinguishers in emergency situations. We frown upon former lovers using the fire extinguisher as a device to smash off a doorknob. Selecting the right tool for the job is as important as how you use that tool. The woman who utilized the fire-fighting device had already left when our officer arrived.

The knob is one of the most important parts of a door latch. It allows interface between the hands of a human and the mechanical heart of the device. It appears that after her Thor-like removal of the knob, it was difficult to turn the latch to enter.

With the woman out of the picture, the officer turned to the man inside the apartment and he was found to be on federal probation. He also smelled of burned, plant-based calming smoke. His probation officer either left that off his list of "Things to avoid," or the man had misread the simple directions included in every box of freedom.

When the officer went to get a camera to document the late night-locksmithing, the man would not let him back into the apartment.

Calls were made to the probation officer and we believe that easily accessible knobs will be missing from future taxpayer-provided housing. So will the herbal supplements.

This story inspired me to return to my roots. Poetry:

Sometimes in life, you are mad at your wife.
She bashes the knob off your door.
She busts up the place and leaves in such haste,
obviously wanting no more.

Since the cops have been called, you meet in the hall.
His nose is more tuned to your weed.
You close-up the door and hide on the floor,
hoping to air out your deed.

The cop he returns. The perp is now burned.
He sees that probation you didst blow.
The feds will return, the cop you will spurn,
but back to the big house you'll go.

I think if the O'Jays were still working their magic, these lyrics would have been a hit.

❋   ❋   ❋

Hitting the building twice with a motor vehicle will cause those inside the building to contact the local gendarme. Upon the arrival of Bangor officers, they discovered the driver was a local lady who wore what any one of us might wear—to bed.

The description in the report was that she was draped with a pink, plush robe and Cheetah-print fuzzy slippers.

Naturally, her dog had come along for the ride. It was a small dog—exactly what you would expect if you were to imagine the kind of dog that a woman wearing a pink robe and cheetah slippers would have along for the ride.

She had been consuming spirits prior to her arrival at the accident scene. She was arrested and charged with Operating Under the Influence. The dog was well cared for at the local shelter for the night. I don't know what else to say.

❋   ❋   ❋

One of our younger sergeants took the complaint of a man

drinking in public. This is not allowed for various reasons. We understand the drinking part. It's the public part that causes an issue.

We suggest looking for more private locations to imbibe, but we are not judging you. We are just giving you free advice based on Maine state statutes.

When the sergeant found the staggering man, he inquired about the fact that the man might have been drinking on someone else's steps. The man told the cop that it was not important because he was "done now, so it doesn't matter." This thinking is logical.

We accept it—not as well as Spock would have, but the sergeant is not a fan of Spock. Not because Spock is a bad person, but because Sarge is more of a realist; and since we are cops, we do the backstroke in the deep Olympic-sized pool of realism.

As a matter of fact, we don't even towel off the realism. We like to "air dry."

The officer asked the man's name, and the man said, "It's illegal for me to tell you my name because then you'll know that I have an arrest warrant for unpaid fines."

This piqued the young realist's interest. The man did not lie. His warrant was active, and he went to jail.

Live long, and prosper, my friend.

* * *

Reports that start with, "A shirtless male approached my cruiser" usually end up with a soundtrack that includes background sound effects featuring tinkling handcuff chains. This one is no different.

The man claimed his shirt had been ripped off by a female as she pulled him out of a cab. She was located by the sound of her voice, which was like a typical voice, but louder and more annoying.

Her speech was slurred, and she approached our officers only to be told that she was far too close. She refused to back away, and, before a true and formal introduction could be facilitated, she was arrested.

She was scrappy, and during the search she was disarmed of her Buck knife as well as a lovely necklace that was not only fashionable but also had a knife attached.

The lady was then taken to jail for the crime of disorderly conduct. She had some experience with the shackles, as she was able to slip them off during the short ride to jail. She was a veritable knife-toting Houdini—only louder.

The shirtless male left the area before we could speak to him again. I would say he was smarter than all of us.

Godspeed, shirtless male. Godspeed.

* * *

While this will never be featured on *Chopped*, we know that to cook an outstanding dish and present it in a fashion that pleases others, you need good kitchen equipment.

A man who disposed of his significant other's liquor stash was contacted by that same significant other and advised that his culinary tools could be recovered from a nearby dumpster.

It seems that the disposal of the spirits caused her to also state that she would be "burning his $#!t!" We don't support this type of conflict resolution.

When he arrived back at his home base, he found that his Crock-Pot, electric frying pan, and four-slice toaster (with a bagel setting) in the dumpster.

His significant other left behind the food chopper. We do not know if this was a message, but we do believe that no meal can start without a base of properly prepared spices and vegetables. Maybe some garlic?

In any event, nothing was burned, so most items are probably usable after a good-wipe down. The case is being investigated.

* * *

A couple of mobile sommeliers did the "sip 'n slip" at Governor's restaurant in Bangor.

The ladies smelled the cork, popped the top, and didn't stop (to pay) before they took the liqufied grapes on a road-trip down Broadway.

Before they left, an employee inquired about them trying to take the wine outside to imbibe, and one of them asked her if she was going to try to stop them.

Talk about the *Grapes of Wrath*—that was naughty!

The "ladies" were found in Old Town by one of their officers. They said the neon lights are bright on Broadway, but on this day, the dim glow of thievery was overcome by the overpowering LEDs of justice.

* * *

The snow has brought out the best in our residents. One of our officers was dispatched to Norfolk Street to try to locate a motor vehicle that was seen towing a person wearing skis. These are the kinds of complaints that our officers love to handle.

We were hopeful to find the adventuresome duo in order to inquire about the best speeds, appropriate rope lengths, and to find out which wax holds up best when applied to skis being used on both hard-packed snow, icy surfaces, and asphalt.

We are not saying that we would not have given them a good dressing down. We are just saying that this is a crime that could call for a complete reenactment. We would do this in a safer venue than the public streets—that is just wrong; but, oh, so right.

The officer could not find the skijoring souls as they had ske-daddled slickly, slipping silently into the snowy shadows. We were sad.

* * *

At 12:16 A.M. our cops were called to a famous breakfast location to speak to a man about his behavior.

When partaking in one of the three most important meals of the day, Americans want to be able to focus exclusively on the eggs and sausage on their own plate. This man made it difficult, as he was showing off his PWL (Personally Worn Lingerie) and rubbing himself in a manner that was not conducive to the full and uninterrupted digestion of a Lumberjack Slam.

We do not judge people by how they look or what they choose to wear. We judge people by what they are doing at the time we encounter them.

I am breaking this down in very simple terms. There are certain words that should never spend time together in one police report. Here are three:
1. Rubbing
2. Breakfast
3. Lingerie

The officer asked the man to move along and gave him a 24-hour criminal trespass warning. The man paid his bill and tipped his server.

These sentences are rife with potential for comedic commentary, but I will remain the prude that I was raised to be.

It should be noted that his waitress was not named Victoria, and we are also keeping the suspect's name a secret.

* * *

A man who liked his Lexus more than life itself was a little upset when the repo man showed up to remove his first love.

For those of you who have dated a woman named Lexus, I am here to inform you that it was not her real name. In this case, we are talking about a car and the man who was in arrears on his payments. Don't do that.

The reallocation specialist had almost completed the loading process when the (now former) owner came running outside and threw a HOAF (Heck of a Fit) as the driver pulled way. The suspect then found himself another set of wheels and pursued in a manner that was unsafe.

The truck driver was now "the hunted."

If I could have added a soundtrack, it would have been "Ride like the Wind" from Christopher Cross—mainly because the chase was so short, and we would have only needed the instrumental introduction to the song. We never would have reached the vocal portion of the '80s classic—Once Cross slides into "It is the night, my body's weak, I'm on the run, no time to sleep," you have to admit, the song loses a little thunder.

The suspect forced the repo man off the road and then blocked the Lexus-laden lorry from moving.

The man yelled and used words that were commonly taught only at Mr. Mephistopheles' School for the Ungifted and Talentless.

The suspect then mounted the flatbed truck to be with his vehicle. The driver could not leave the scene safely since he now had a passenger that was as unwelcome as a tick on an anemic hound dog.

The driver called for law enforcement assistance.

The officer arrived and interviewed the suspect, who told him that he had actually been in the car when it was repo'd. This was not true; that is, unless the driver of the offending and currently empty chase vehicle had slipped over the grassy knoll prior to the arrival of the po-po.

The man was issued a summons for driving to endanger, and the Lexus left in the hands of the repo company.

* * *

A man who found himself in need of wise counsel or a locksmith, called for the police. We do provide wise counsel from time to time, but our locksmithing tools consist of items that can only break windows, not repair broken hearts.

The man was found to be standing, forlorn, on the front steps of an Ohio Street address. He informed the officer that he had received a text from his "soon-to-be former girlfriend" indicating that she believed he was a liar.

He advised the officer that he had lived there for two months but today returned home to find himself on the outside with his belongings on the inside. The door had been purposefully locked.

When the officer Doctor Phil'd his way into the details, he found out that the woman had discovered—just today—that the chilly and now-lonely man was a registered sex offender.

She indicated that he had been less than truthful with her and that he needed to find a new place to call his own. We assume his dishonesty centered around the fact that he "forgot" to mention his registered-sex-offender status. We do understand that it is not something one would place in their Tinder profile.

The cop advised the man that he would need to abide by the woman's wishes and that he was no longer included in her "wish list."

TC's Maxim #29192: "When life gives you lemons, many times it is because you deserved them."

*   *   *

One of our new officers was sent to a United States Post Office mailbox near Center Street to take the report of a suspicious incident.

Several people reported seeing a man reaching into the big blue mailbox, or at least trying, and then putting unknown items back inside the box. In this day and age, we appreciate calls like this, and we investigated immediately.

We located an authorized U.S. Postal Service employee who had a set of keys and aided them in removing the following items from the mailbox:

One can of Stokley's smooth sliced carrots, a jar of Natural Smooth Nut'n Better peanut butter, and one half-pint carton of Dairy Pure.

Knowing full well that there is a $250,000 fine (and the possibility of federal imprisonment for up to three years) for tampering with a United States Postal Service mailbox (Title 18, United States Code, Section 1705), we are looking for a thin man, about 5'10", wearing neon mittens and a scarf.

While looking around the area afterward, the officer surmised that almost everyone he saw was sturdier-built, wearing Carhartt jackets, Muck boots, and old Wells-Lamont gloves. This *is* Maine.

After returning to the station, he came to the conclusion that the suspect was most likely an athletic man who was lactose intolerant, without a peanut allergy, and who has 20/20 vision; he's watched *NCIS*.

Due to the mention of neon mittens and scarf, the officer is checking the local ski areas. The case is still under investigation.

*   *   *

The hospital security team explained to our officer that a man pushed a woman away from their facility using a stolen wheelchair, and it was clear that they were not in need of the conveyance. The couple headed away from the hospital at a rapid pace, refusing to stop at the beckoning call from the guardians of the healthcare galaxy.

Shortly thereafter, the officer noted a lone occupant of a wheelchair doing wheelies and spinning in circles in the parking lot of a local pharmacy. It was midnight.

Since the female former occupant of the wheelchair was nowhere to be seen, the officer had to use only the large block letters painted across the back of the chair for confirmation that this was his suspect vehicle.

The officer approached the non-debilitated half of the not-so-disabled dynamic duo and introduced himself. The man stood up quickly and apologized for what he had done. He promised to return the chair to its rightful owner so that it could again be used to help those in need.

Since the man was intoxicated and obviously contrite about his sins, the cop told him that he would not charge him with the theft, but would instead arrest him on an outstanding warrant. The man was dismayed but determined to face his demons with an apologetic tone.

Security staff quickly came to the scene to pick up their chair and gaze upon the man in a manner that would indicate their disappointment in his actions.

Security staff are trained worldwide with this "disappointed look," and it is a practical and useful tool that has been passed down from parents, grandparents, and high school assistant principals.

This man needed more than a distasteful stare; he was a man who needed a good dose of a knitted-brow stink-eye and the appropriate application of handcuffs.

During a subsequent search of his person, the officer discovered that the man had secreted away several Suboxone strips that did not belong to him. This added the charge of possession of schedule W drugs to the man's arrest sheet.

The woman had walked away prior to his arrest, which made it fairly clear that neither of them needed a wheelchair in the first place.

These times do try us. My penchant for simple poetry was revived when I wrote this. I felt the need to alliterate:

Wandering whippersnappers wheelbarrowing whimsically away from watchmen were discovered during the witless display of wheelies and widdershins. Wisenheimer with wanderlust was under influence of whiskey and schedule W drugs. We await words with wife.

Wow, just wow.

*　*　*

Two of our officers were sent to a Central Street eatery to attempt to locate a man wearing khaki pants and a button-up shirt.

We have no rules against wearing either khakis or dress shirts. The men and women of the Bangor Police Department appreciate a sharp-dressed man, or woman. Since a neatly pressed pair of khakis is a universally acceptable manner of dress for both men and women alike, we certainly appreciate that this man was representing all good khaki wearers everywhere.

The issue really was that the man had been beating on the windows of the restaurant with a broom. This is not khaki-like behavior.

He also allegedly called the folks inside the building a bunch of "cop-calling f#$%&@s." He spoke the truth, except for the F-bomb turned noun. That was just mean. They had called the police. We encourage it. They only mentioned that he was wearing khakis because that's what people do. They describe you by what you are wearing.

The violent broom-play was not appropriate; that is unless you are curling.

In that case, f-bombs can only be hurled at opponents during the icy heat of battle. Kind Canadians do not appreciate that type of unsportsmanlike conduct and I believe they might drag you out behind the arena for a quick lesson in Canadian kindness.

A short time after the first call, patrol officers located a man carrying a broom while walking on the State Street hill. He was wearing khakis and a button-up shirt. Oddly, he denied the behaviors that I previously described.

The officers have been around long enough to know that if it wears khakis and carries a broom, it quite possibly could be the same person who was seen smashing the window and using foul language.

The man denied any wrongdoing, but did not have a really good reason to be carrying a broom.

Everyone knows that the summer Quidditch season ends in July, and since that time, we have not seen much random brooms-man-ship around town.

After checking their law books, it was discovered that there was no law in effect that prohibits the casual and open carry of a broom, or even a mop.

He was given a disorderly conduct warning and told that if someone called again, we would be placing him under arrest and putting his broom into the evidence closet. Of course, the broom would probably fall down several times, causing us to open the door to stand it back up, because brooms sometimes have a mind of their own.

We would have probably had to change the name on the evidence closet once we put a broom inside. This would have only caused more work for us. So we let him take his broom and be on his way.

*   *   *

While the world might see our job as glamorous, you should know that any officer with a modicum of experience will not shiver with delight when sent to speak to a person in a blue tank top and blonde ponytail. In high school, there would have been a rush to find someone fitting that description. As a police officer, not so much.

Since most of us have had the pleasure of riding the express train to reality, we know full well that things are never what they seem or even what we hope they will be.

The conductor on that train wears a yellow leisure suit and keeps his floral-patterned nylon shirt buttoned up as far as his xiphoid process. How else would we see his Avon arrowhead necklace?

We know full well that the person we are being sent to investigate will more than likely be drunk and possibly out looking for his former dream ride—a 1980 Trans Am; the one with the turbo 301 cubic-inch engine and automatic transmission. That's right; like a blue tank top on an intoxicated man, the 1980 Trans-Am was never a cool choice.

Once Pontiac removed the manual transmission and the 6.6-liter cast-iron block of American freedom from the T-A, it suddenly became clear that Burt Reynolds was wearing a hair piece, and Sally Field didn't even want to take his hat off.

For the rest of us? We thanked the good lord for the power of the Avon arrowhead necklace and a Zayre's bag full of Brut cologne.

The suspect in question had been yelling at the store clerk as she told him that the bathroom was out of service. The water had been turned off. This was upsetting to him. He then began to yell at other patrons. This makes people uncomfortable. We are used to uncomfortable situations and relish an opportunity to make them better.

When the man threw his beer and donuts on the counter— no, I did not make that part up—in an attempt to make a purchase, she told him that he could buy the donuts but she would not sell him any more intoxicants. This went over like the passing of gas in a house of worship.

While it was evident the man was a Homer Simpson fan, he still left without the donuts.

The officers located the man and gave him a criminal trespass warning and informed him that he could not return to the store for a period of one year. He said he was sorry for acting out and apologized. Officers did not make any fashion suggestions for future outings.

* * *

A gentleman in North Carolina was scouring the interweb to find a suitable companion from an Asian dating website. He considers this activity a type of research. We call it "surfing porn."

During his "research," he discovered an image of a woman of apparent Asian descent. She was tied to a tree. This was a photo and not a video, which is important to note since he believed the activity was in progress.

He had used several types of math, along with Google Earth,

and decided that the woman was currently in Bangor, and he gave us the coordinates.

Not in a position to argue about something that could be this serious, we sent an officer to the location the man had deduced might hold clues to the whereabouts of the woman.

The cop found a parking lot with no trees. It should be noted that the woman was not there either.

The man was informed that his calculations were not correct and that we appreciated his help. We suspect that he returned to his research.

Our belief is that the website has multiple photographs of individuals in other precarious situations, and, while not passing judgement, we suspect that some of the images might be contrived or staged for theatrical purposes; these are fine, fine actors.

We also would like to point out that there are trees in many locations around our great United States and that this, one, defining characteristic should not always make you think of Maine—unless it's a white pine; that is our state tree.

* * *

Blazin' up a fatty while scrubbing your dirties might seem like a superb and supreme way to pass the time until the Tide Pods do the job for which they were intended; we get it.

On a nice day at the laundromat, you might even want to step outside, hop in the driver's seat of your Sentra, and select one of many fine radio stations serving the greater-Bangor region—bad idea. People call us about those things, and we then have to stop by. No one really wants to see us; we know this.

A bunch of quarters, a Tide pod, an iPod, and fresh bud can equal a relaxed outlook on the day. The issue is that "smoking the weed" is not an approved public activity.

Now, before you get all "you're killin' me with your rules and stomping my buzz," I understand. One of the specific rules of our new-found freedom was that marijuana was not supposed to be smoked in public or in the driver's seat.

Getting behind the wheel with a stick of fiery delightfulness is not approved. Please just follow the rules, and we will just wave on our way by to the pastry shop. Maybe we will see you there.

The man in his car enjoying the sunbeam was very understanding and did not realize it was a bad idea. He had to go throw his stuff in the dryer, so we didn't stay long. No, he was not summoned, just warned.

Rules—ruining everything since the beginning of time.

* * *

1:04 A.M. is well past the time your mom wanted you home—and for good reason. Our officers found themselves in Abbot Square with a couple of boys who were determined to face-off in an epic battle of strength.

Untanned, untoned, and uncovered, the man-babies stripped to their skins in order to signal to the world that there was a bare-chested throw-down about to take place.

Shirts were tossed aside by both participants. This is fun to watch; we cannot lie. (Tossing aside an article of clothing prior to a throw-down is an ancient practice first utilized when our Neanderthal forbears tossed aside heavy, smelly animal skins because they got in the way of a good old-fashioned donnybrook).

Yes, even the new light-blue, counterfeit Costa-branded shirt, which one of the men had picked up at a discount (two-for-one) price during a visit to one of the transient sellers who purveyed this and other fine counterfeit clothing during Maine's late-summer run of state fairs.

Fried dough? Games of chance? Drunken tomfoolery out behind the broken Zipper ride?

This shirt, in all its fakery, had been utilized to entice numerous ladies into talking to the lad during similar late-night forays to nightclubs and karaoke bars in our area.

On one such occasion, he had been called out by an astute and somewhat fashion-conscious maiden when she noted that he had forgotten to remove the nine-dollar price tag from just under the sleeve of the Shark-Week-inspired sportswear.

Everyone knows that nine bucks doesn't get you a genuine Costa, even if the lack of proper laundering can give the 60/40 blend a subtle odor of baitfish and saltwater.

Regardless of the shirts they were now not wearing, the fight was about to go down.

Our officers intervened with bright lights and loud voices to warn the inebriated, pay-per-view-trained Mixed Martial Arts standouts to stop this nonsense immediately.

Our navy-blue-clad vocalized intervention was enough to turn the imaginary octagon into an open-air honeymoon suite that would give any cheesy Pocono newlywed resort a run for its money. No, there was no heart-shaped pool, but if you squinted a bit you might have believed the concrete curbing to be a dull-colored foam pool noodle.

The two men seemed relieved that the fight would be cancelled due to our attendance. Suddenly, without warning, they embraced in a hug that can only be described as touching.

Sweaty, beer-stained delight ensued. It seems that the men had been friends for a long, long time.

The blows, which were no longer imminent, had turned to embosomed affection for one another.

While you suspected this would turn into a first-class, full-fledged melee due to the arrival of police officers, just the opposite happened. These are the stories that will never be carried on the national networks.

Well, maybe the Hallmark Channel. Of course, the actors would be clothed and more attractive.

The bros walked off into the night, but not before picking up their shirts and checking for obvious signs of dust, dirt, and long-forgotten dangling price tags. These could be worn again, soon, in their quest to get someone to bring a milkshake to their yard.

The ladies in our city expect no less.

* * *

To the individual who lost your mom's good pillowcase in the night deposit box at a local financial institution, we have it in evidence.

We urge you to stop by the police department to claim the case.

In our experience, there are far better ways to secure funding for future projects; a job is one, a loan from a close friend, a job, collecting returnables, or, a job.

The pillowcase-attached-to-fishing-line trick never works.

We suspect that the fishing line broke during your border-line genius attempt to withdraw cash and would like to discuss the activity with you at your earliest convenience.

The remnant of your fishing line appears to be a low-grade monofilament.

I would have gone with braided line, but I also know that it still would not have been successful for a myriad of reasons, none of which I can share here, as I have been cautioned against using words that might damage the feelings of ne'er-do-wells and miscreants—not that I would consider you to be one of those aforementioned monikers.

P.S: If you are a mom who has suddenly noticed a pillowcase missing from the linen closet, contact us with a description and maybe we can turn your dream of moving that kid out of your basement into a reality. It would make a perfect sewing or craft room.

P.S.S: If you are a fisherman who has a child living in the basement and he/she recently asked for a short piece of fishing line and was holding a pillowcase, you should also call us.

* * *

A man who carpet-bombed two of our officers with the mother of all expletives would not stop yelling inside a respectable retail establishment. A crowd gathered and watched.

That's what crowds do.

We don't blame them, as our uniforms have provided us with front row seats to the wackiest show on earth. We urge folks to make themselves familiar with the ongoing fracas in all three rings. Lean in if you cannot see clearly.

Just as your grandmother could prepare and present leftovers in many different ways, the drooling and spitting man was able to make the f-bomb into a smorgasbord of swearing, a casserole of cursing, and a bucket of blasphemy. There was no end to his vicious vitriol, and he was ordered to leave.

He was first asked to sign the criminal trespass order, and refused. He walked down the sidewalk and ended up at a laundromat.

With no intention of cleaning up his act, he continued his loud and obnoxious behavior, and the management asked him to leave. He refused.

Even the well-maintained commercial-grade washers could not have cleansed this man's potty-mouth. We considered washing and folding him, but the per-pound rate was far more than the officer had on his person.

The man was then arrested and charged with criminal trespass. On the way to jail, the conversation went as expected. The
man told the officer that he was going to bite him. The officer
asked him not to do that. He did not.

TC's Maxim #23: Our patience is a virtue, but it comes with a
curfew.

* * *

A woman who came forward to share important drug information
told the officer that she wanted to help clear the city of drug deal-
ers who were killing our youth.

Upon further questioning, the lady told the officer that she
knew where they were selling crack right at that very moment.

The officer asked how she knew for sure. She told him that
she had just bought a substantial amount of crack and had smoked
all of it before she called.

He thanked her for the information and told her that he
would speak to her later when she was not so high.

He did slide her a "pro-tip" by explaining that when she buys
from the crack dealer, it increases his profits, thus helps keep him
in business. She had not taken that into consideration in her campaign to clear Bangor of illegal substances.

* * *

Bangor officers were dispatched to an east-side apartment
building for a complaint of loud noises. During the investigation,
officers stood outside the apartment in question but heard no
noises at all.

This happens in both cartoons and in real life. Sometimes

we feel that we are just characters in a cartoon that the kids really should not be watching.

After knocking on the door, officers were greeted by a very friendly—and naked—man. Nudity, in the privacy of one's own home, is not a surprise to any police officer, but we would always rather citizens come to the door in at least a robe, towel, or even a curtain. Aprons make us laugh and properly placed pizza boxes will elicit a full-on chortle or guffaw.

We get it—it's your house. A man's home is his castle, and if that man wants to roam the grounds wearing nothing but a smile, we understand. We just don't need to see the plumbing.

The man invited them in, and the officers entered with the expectation that they might discover who had been making all that racket. While keeping their eyes above shoulder level, they surveyed the sparsely furnished room.

What they found inside the home was perplexing. The man was naked and alone. However, he was not naked and afraid as was evidenced by his cordial reaction to the officers.

The man admitted that a woman he knew quite well had just left and that she could have been the one responsible for the noise that was reported. The officers asked him to keep any further noise to a minimum and to keep some pants around in case their presence was requested again. The man said he would do just that.

* * *

Officers were sent to a Main Street hotel to remove a loud group of revelers from their room. The group had been warned to quiet down multiple times.

You should know that people do not always comply with requests from hoteliers.

Many in the group had selected "L-28" on the glass-front, full-view vending machine just down the hall. It's just to the left of the ice machine. Pressing those magic buttons apparently dispenses a law degree (focusing mainly on the rights of those who party loudly) along with complimentary breath mints, which smell exactly like cheap wine and warm, domestic beer.

At least two of the ladies also punched in "A-32." For $1.75, you get an instant megaphone-like voice, and you immediately believe you are on *The Jerry Springer Show*. For an additional two dollars, you can get a voice changing device that makes your voice sound exactly like Teresa from *The Real Housewives of New Jersey*. Thank the good lord that they ran out of change.

The standard battle cry of "We are not leaving," was heard and not one single "inside voice" was detected.

Cell phone batteries were rapidly drained as those individuals moved down the hall in a bevy of belligerence. Filming the cops is the new middle finger. In fact, if you film us properly, you can keep your middle finger up as a support to your iPhone. It takes practice but can be done. I have seen it.

It should be noted that filming the police is completely legal and accepted.

Avoid hitting us with the phone. You will go from being the next James Cameron to "San Quentin" Tarantino in an instant, for that is assault. Practice on your friends.

Back to our story.

The multiple cop-film close-ups and entertaining knave-like narratives would make the cinematography of the *Blair Witch Project* seem like an outdoor scene from *Naked and Afraid*.

The epic closing scene at the hotel desk called for extras, and we brought ladies and gentlemen from the Bangor Police Department Screen Actors' Guild. They were already in full costume.

In the end, two of the ladies were taken to our remote studio location on Hammond Street. Complimentary glamour shots were taken and charges of disorderly conduct and obstructing government administration were documented.

The previews of this film are not appropriate for those under the age of seventeen.

* * *

Our officer was called to a Hammond Street apartment building to settle a dispute between neighbors. For those of you who have never had the pleasure of trying to settle a dispute between neighbors: Do not try this at home.

A man was complaining that his neighbor was pounding on the walls so hard his pictures were falling onto the floor.

The cop attempted to speak to the offending individual and was met with the following quote. "It is F$*^@$! P!@#*# like you, harassing people like me, that Americans are sick of and are killing you."

The officer quickly reviewed the many Sunday school lessons that were seared into his memory, and he could not recall this particular statement in the good book. His chosen house of worship did not contain the "bad book," so he supposed that it might be something he had missed on that Sunday back in the summer of 1987, when he had feigned sickness in order to watch reruns of *Miami Vice*, mostly for fashion tips.

The cop also avoided trying to correct the grammatical make-up of the suspect's sentence. He was clearly not a welcome visitor in the hallway and felt that getting out his virtual red pen of correction would only cause the F-bombing beast to become angrier. The officer recalled that his wife had told him that "only the snake of spite spews such venom at people with a penchant for promoting peace." He loves that woman.

He recalled a passage that started with "blessed are the peacemakers," but, in this case, he was going to choose the Colt model over the Beatitudes. He told the man to immediately stop yelling, swearing, banging on the walls, and generally being a jerk to the others in the building, or he would be taking him to jail with no regard for the man's schedule or lunch and dinner plans.

The loud and generally obnoxious neighbor began to throttle back and said, "Okay, okay, okay, just f$&*#@% stop threatening me and leave the property. This is why people are killing people like you."

The officer felt like there was a small breakthrough, but was not going to be writing this man a recommendation to divinity school. He noted that the man smelled of intoxicants and had obviously been partaking of wine that "moveth in the cup." He was going to relay to the man that it meant "fermented," but decided to tell him to cork it immediately and be gone from his sight.

He then told the man if he uttered one more word, even if it was kind, he would be taking him to jail. The man went back into his apartment and was not heard from again that day.

Unlike Orkin, we cannot guarantee that pest removal is permanent. Sometimes they quiet down and sometimes we take them to the county jail and hope that the criminal justice system can change the long-term behavior of annoying individuals.

If we were able to exchange old neighbors for new neighbors and provide a guarantee, we would become the most popular people working under the Municipal Services Umbrella (MSU).

We do not offer "loaner neighbors." Long-term issues are sometimes only solved through a good landlord/tenant partnership.

TC's Maxim #94382: Police action is sometimes just a Band-Aid, when what you really need is a hip replacement.

* * *

A man who went to a fast food drive-thru requested a small order of French fries. This is not a significant event.

Again, I write these words with the intent that they can be enjoyed by most members of the modern family. The manner in which this man requested the French fries was very rude.

The man, who longed for deep-fried potatoes (presented in a recyclable container), told the drive-thru representative that he wanted "a small F*&$ing French fry, now!"

I don't know about you, but my momma would have smacked those words out of my mouth so fast that I would have been begging for extra salt to heal the wounds that were left behind where my lips had formerly been located.

The manager overheard the manner in which the order was placed and took control of the headset and microphone for the purpose of informing the potato-pirate that he would not be served due to his language and attitude. This manager would not allow his employees to be treated in such a disrespectful manner, and we salute him for trying to make America more polite.

The foul-mouthed seeker of salty spuds marched into the restaurant and continued to be rude and disrespectful. He then struck the cash register in an attempt to petrIfy the serveIs just before he marched out, sans fries.

The registration number on his vehicle allowed officers to find him rather quickly and discuss the incident. The man was issued a criminal trespass notice that banned him from visiting that drive-thru for the next 364 days. Got fries? Nope, not today.

5.

The Cop

"The Cop" is a series of stories about an unnamed police officer. The stories are fictional, but are based on real people and real experiences.

Banana Bread

He stopped, mainly to check on her. The banana bread was purely a secondary reason, but it easily could have been the primary reason.

Sandwiched between his concerns for her frailty and the fact that winter was here was still the fact that she used pecans in the warm loaves of bread. She always had cream cheese. Butter was fine, but the cream cheese—it was like icing on the cake, or, at least, cream cheese on the banana bread.

He knew her age, but he never confronted her when she lied about it. If the Department of Motor Vehicle database was correct, there were ten years separating her from her fibs. She was ninety-one, but she could have passed for a young seventy-five.

Since her husband had passed away in 2014, she had become his personal project. Not every week, but at least every few weeks, he would stop by and drop off treats for the cat or some bananas. Two days later, he would reap the benefits of the discount fruit from South America.

If the snow was falling, he would pull in and scrape off her porch and the steps, throw down a little sand for traction, and then finish out his tour with a coffee and maybe a newspaper. He still read the newspaper, or at least the classifieds. He really wanted a motorhome.

He had spoken to her daughter in Memphis a few times. She called him to say thank you for taking the time to check on her mom. She also told him the time was coming for her to move to Memphis. Mother would hear nothing of it; she was fine. She had grown up in much tougher conditions than were present in the side-hall cape on the even-numbered side of the tree-lined street where she had raised two children.

He heard a muffled groan from inside the doorway. It was still dark, but he knew exactly what had happened. The hallway led to the living room, just off to the right. He tried the knob, and she had done what he had told her to do so many times when he found it open. She had finally locked it. He shone his flashlight into the foyer, and he saw what he knew he would see sooner or later.

The key was where they had agreed it to be, not under the mat. The nail under the porch was easy to reach. The key, spray painted black to keep it from being easily seen, hung exactly where he had placed it two years ago.

The cold brass was a welcome feeling as he turned the old lock and swung open the door. He had already radioed for the paramedics. He hated sirens; they were always too loud, and he had had his fill of them. Tonight, they were melodious. The winter air allowed the noise to travel the two miles to Central. They would be here soon.

He turned on the light and knew from her position that something was broken. Her hands were cold but her pulse was strong. He grabbed a blanket and pillow from the couch that she never sat on and then wrapped her up.

On the way to the hospital, the medics told him that it was a pretty good chance she had broken her hip. She opened her eyes a little and motioned for him to come closer to her oxygen mask. He leaned over quickly, never letting go of her hand.

Her voice was weak but clear. "If I had known you were coming, I would have baked you something." He laughed; she just smirked.

After getting her settled at the hospital, he had one of the guys pick him up in order to drop him off at her house to get his cruiser.

He fed and watered the cat, turned the heat back to sixty degrees, and made sure that the house was secure. The bananas on the counter were just over-ripe enough for banana bread. He was pretty sure that he wouldn't taste it again unless he got a good deal on a flight to Tennessee.

And so it goes in the life of a cop.

Keep your hands to yourself, leave other people's things alone, and be kind to one another.

Check on your neighbors and loved ones a little bit more this year. We are all getting older.

Eggs

The summer, which had been much anticipated for most, was another summer of the same sadness for the boy, Ronnie.

The school year was a respite from spending too much time at home with his drunken stepfather and painkiller-addicted mother. They loved him the best way they knew how; that's what the school counselor told him.

He loved them too—at least until they were able to get the next bottle or fix. Then he hated them for a time. He read as much as he could in the room he shared with his sister. He loved her unconditionally. He couldn't imagine ever hating her. They walked to the public library together several days a week.

She was a pretty girl and wasn't saddled with his physical traits. Her dad wasn't his dad, and it was easy to see the difference in their appearance. He never knew his real dad, but he hated him when he looked in the mirror.

She was three years younger. He was already worried for her when he finally found a way to leave—for anywhere, as soon as he could. His dream was to take her with him.

It was a pipe dream.

Ronnie sweltered while his friends, acquaintances, and sworn junior-high-school enemies attended summer camps and went on interesting family vacations. In their down time, they went to the lake. The public beaches just outside of his reach in the towns around Bangor were inviting, but he was never invited.

He had been to Green Lake a couple of times when his step-dad was feeling generous—and sober enough to drive them there.

Ronnie made his own shorts from a pair of pants that were too short for him anyway. He used scissors that he found on the porch. Rusted shut, he hit them repeatedly with the trickling spray from a rusty-bottomed can of WD-40. He whacked them against the concrete basement wall to make them operable for the dull-cut just above the worn-out knees of his former "school jeans."

He paid no mind to his rapid growth spurt while he was try-ing to sneak through his seventh-grade year unnoticed. He didn't realize his good jeans were too short. He didn't need to; his en-emies did. They pointed it out at lunch and on the walks home.

He soaked up the insults with a steel inner core, invisible to those who didn't know that fortitude doesn't come pre-packaged with a clear label. He took the comments in stride as he knew that eighth grade was going to be better.

The cops were always at the apartment house; remarkably, not for his family. They were poor, alcohol addled, and want-ing for much, but his stepdad was not a violent drunk. His mom stayed in bed most of the time. He cooked for his sister, mostly eggs and toast. They loved eggs, and it was a good thing they did. His Aunt Rhonda had backyard chickens and made sure the fridge always had milk, bread, and eggs—lots of eggs.

Aunt Rhonda sometimes brought vegetables from her gar-den. She bought Ronnie two new pairs of jeans and a couple of discount-rack tee shirts for his summer wardrobe. No one could have been prouder in a Coca-Cola tee shirt from a discontinued promotional campaign. He felt that it could be acceptable due to its "retro" feel. He knew it was a pipe dream, too.

Another loud, banging dispute between the downstairs neighbors brought the cops again. He and his sister were eating breakfast, at lunchtime. Eggs, always eggs.

The cops came; voices were raised; voices became quieter. He heard a deep-voiced cop warning the neighbors to quiet down or someone would be arrested. The cop was firm, but he sounded kind. Ronnie put down his fork, walked down the stairs, and went out on the porch to catch a glimpse of the face belonging to the cop with the deep voice.

Ronnie sat in the green nylon-webbed lawn chair overlooking the overgrown weeds that the landlord claimed was a lawn. Round bullseye-shaped burns in the arms and webbing drew the eye toward the right side of the chair, where a tin can sitting on the gray porch floor held hundreds of cigarette butts. He swore he would never smoke, but he was tempted sometimes, out of boredom.

He heard heavy footsteps coming through the common hallway, and he expected to see the big man with the big voice. His face must have exuded surprise as a short, thin, young cop stepped out into the daylight. Ronnie stared, then looked away quickly when the cop spoke to him in a booming voice.

"How are you son?" Ronnie tried to answer, "Good," but it didn't come out. For some reason, he was unnerved and surprised that the voice didn't fit his earlier, invisible, impression. The cop smiled. He had seen Ronnie between here and the small corner market over on Hammond Street many times. The boy was always walking with a younger girl.

"How's your sister this summer?"

Ronnie was bewildered that the cop knew he had a sister. "She's good. Eating lunch, upstairs."

The cop walked closer. "What's for lunch?"

Ronnie said, "Eggs. Eggs with green pepper. I cooked it."

The cop smiled wider. "Are you a good cook?"

Ronnie made eye contact for the first time. "I think I am. I don't burn them."

"So, a green pepper omelet?"

"No," Ronnie replied quickly. "An omelet has cheese, and I didn't have any cheese."

The cop leaned against the chipped and faded porch rail. "You need cheese for an omelet? I had no idea you couldn't call it an omelet without cheese. What kind do you like?"

Ronnie didn't understand the question because he didn't eat that much cheese. "Any kind, I guess."

The cop was wise to why Ronnie didn't have any cheese. He asked the boy if he wanted a police badge sticker. Ronnie said, "Can I get one for my sister, too?"

The cop said, "Of course you can. I'll tell you what, I will give you five because that's all I have in my pocket. You can use them, put them on a bike, give one to your sister, and just save the rest for later."

Ronnie reached out and took the blue and silver stickers, careful not to squeeze and bend them.

"Next time I come by, I'll bring cheese. If eggs can't be an omelet without cheese, then I don't want to be responsible for your sister not getting a proper omelet."

Ronnie smiled. "You don't have to do that. My Aunt Rhonda brings us the eggs. And the peppers from her garden."

The cop stayed for a few more minutes. He showed Ronnie and his sister the inside of the cruiser. The hard-plastic back seat was always a hit. Ronnie didn't want to sit in the driver's seat but pushed his sister toward the car when she balked at the idea as well. She sat inside and held the steering wheel, clicked the spotlight on and off too many times, and hit the siren button when the deep-voiced cop told her it was okay.

The radio squawked again, and the cop had to leave quickly.

Later that day, he checked the computer for law enforcement contact with Ronnie's family; there was very little. Only a few confidential requests from a lady named Rhonda from Hermon. She was worried that the kids were raising themselves. Digging deeper, he could see that Human Services was well aware of the issues and that a caseworker was also assigned to the family.

He dropped off two packages of Sargento Swiss cheese slices about a week later. Ronnie thanked him with a huge smile.

"Let me know if that makes the eggs into an omelet!"

Ronnie waved back at him as he ran up the old steps to the porch, disappearing quickly into the house.

Late August brought the opening of school. The deep-voiced cop saw all the kids from his beat as they were walking back and forth. He waved at all of them. Some looked away, some waved back. Still, he waved, as he knew that's just about all he could do for most of them.

Two weeks into September, he saw Ronnie with his sister walking toward home. He pulled up and gave the air horn two short taps. Happy-taps were an art. Too long and it was scary, too many seemed angry. He had practiced happy-taps, and his index finger could pull it off just about every single time.

The kids turned and Ronnie broke into a smile as the short, deep-voiced cop pulled up beside them and rolled down his passenger-side window.

"How was the omelet?"

The little girl peered back from behind Ronnie's faded blue backpack. He could see that she was smiling.

Ronnie said, "The omelets were good."

"How's your Aunt Rhonda?"

Ronnie wondered how the cop remembered so much. "She's good. She is still bringing eggs and lots of zucchini. I've even put that into the omelets."

The cop laughed, as he knew the scourge of a strong crop of zucchini. In Maine, the green gourd was placed into everything, used heavily until the last of it was gone. Zucchini bread, zucchini muffins, zucchini cake, pickled zucchini, fried zucchini, and, of course blanched zucchini. Ronnie was doing his part by including it in the omelets.

The cop could see that Ronnie's sister had badge stickers on her book bag and her lunchbox. Ronnie didn't have any on his gear. The cop didn't mention it. He didn't know of any eighth grader who would have a badge sticker that would be visible to their friends.

"I like your Coca-Cola tee shirt, that's sharp!"

Ronnie smiled again and said, "Thanks!'

The cop beeped the horn again and slowly drove away.

The duo waved and kept walking toward home. Ronnie looked forward to the day when he could be somewhere else, but for now he needed to take care of things here.

"What do you want for supper?" he asked as he smoothed down the badge sticker on her book bag.

She thought for a moment and looked up at her big brother and said, "How about French toast?" He shook his head up and down to indicate that it wasn't a bad idea.

He had grown about two more inches this past summer and he had not heard nearly as much from last year's bullies. He chalked up the growth to plenty of eggs but felt that the cheese might have given him a boost, as well.

Maybe this year would be better than the last. They walked home silently, together.

Provolone

The old man would never accept a sandwich. He would just turn his nose up and walk away. He had no interest in speaking to the cop. While their conversations were short and not very friendly, the cop felt that he should keep trying. Sometimes the old man might say hello; some nights he would just stare.

He would never accept food. The cop had offered repeatedly for weeks. The man's sneakers had duct tape wrapped around the toes to keep them from becoming flip-flops. If he wouldn't take a sandwich, he certainly wouldn't take a pair of shoes.

The cop drove down Water Street and wheeled over to the waterfront. It was 0233. He opened the sandwich that he had picked up at 2100. The oil had soaked into the roll and made eating a slippery prospect. The rectangular white cheese was not provolone. Provolone is not rectangular. No cheese should be rectangular. He always asked for provolone, and he never got it.

The good news was that his tie (which was good for exactly nothing) caught the cheese before it landed on his shirt. The coating of oil allowed it to slide halfway down the black polyester choking device. His tie bar stopped the slice of white cheese, if it was cheese, dead in its tracks.

He pulled off the clip-on. The cheese adhered nicely. He shook it out the open window, and the cheese disappeared. He pulled the tie back inside and threw it into the duty-bag strapped to the passenger seat.

Sergeant Stuart probably wouldn't even notice. If the cop stayed out of the station like he was supposed to, he wouldn't encounter "Stewie" until he went in to finish up paperwork around 0515. By then, the Sarge wouldn't be wearing his tie either.

The tide in the Penobscot River was going out. Some folks were tucked away in their boats down on the city dock. He could hear a few boisterous voices now and then, but as he sat quietly finishing the sandwich, the voices from the boats became softer. The lights went out. He thought to himself that they must be out of beer.

WKIT was playing the Rolling Stones. This was a good sign. "Beast of Burden" reminded him of his time when he raked blueberries in high school and college. Those were long, hot summers. Tonight his biggest problem was no provolone. It had been slow—no calls and no drunk drivers. His most dangerous encounter had been the old homeless man who still wouldn't take the handout of a sandwich.

He pulled a Granny Smith apple from his duty bag. He snagged the last two on the way out the door tonight while heading to roll call. Naturally, this one was bruised. It was too dark inside the Ford to notice the brown spots.

He pulled the Crown Vic's gear selector to "D" and took the slow drive back toward Pickering Square. People were finally clearing out. Two characters were playing hacky sack near the fountain. One obviously inebriated traveler was slouching on a bench. And there, leaning against a tiny decorative maple tree, stood the old man with the duct tape on his shoes.

He slow-rolled to a stop, as close to the man as he dared. The old man looked away. The cop thought to himself that the man must live or sleep nearby. The core of the apple was all he had left in his hand. He turned down the radio and put the cruiser in park. He got out of the car to throw the core away in the overflowing steel trash can. His toss landed it right on top until the cleanly gnawed apple corpse slid off a ketchup-stained French fry box and landed on the ground. He stooped to pick it up, a little embarrassed that he was not a better shot. He heard the old man snicker.

This was a start, he thought to himself.

The old man watched him as he walked back to the car. He adjusted his duty belt and made a decision to eat more apples and fewer crappy sandwiches.

As he got back in his car, the old man said, "I like apples." He got in and shut the door. He was lost for words for a moment. He reached his right hand over the computer monitor and pulled out the second Granny Smith. He transferred it to his left hand and held it up, "You are in luck." He held it out the window.

The old man covered the fifteen feet at a fairly quick pace. The duct tape held. He gingerly took the apple out of the cop's hand and displayed his yellow teeth in what could have been described as a smile. Even though there were very few teeth involved, it was obvious the man was pleased.

The cop put the car in drive and checked the computer monitor—still no calls for service. He looked back at the man who had returned to the small, decorative maple. He had put the apple in his pocket and was leaning back against the tree. The old man yelled out, "Looks like a piece of cheese on your door." The cop smiled and hollered back, "That's not cheese!"

He pulled out onto Washington Street as the Doobies sang "Black Water." He headed to the car wash at the motor pool.

For the first time in weeks, he was glad they'd forgotten the provolone.

Rabbit with a Badge

The digital clock on the dash remained silent as the internal components worked collectively to gain another thirteen minutes and twenty-two seconds in order to reach the magic number of 0300.

His eyelids felt as if they were laden with lead weights, and he removed his glasses to rub his eyes while the cool spring wind snuck through the partially lowered passenger-side window to swirl about for a moment, just before exiting out the rear driver side window.

Fifty-seven miles per hour down I-95 to the Hammond Street exit created a man-made tempest inside the Taurus as the pages in his summons book danced delightfully on top of the duty bag seat-belted to the passenger seat. His ball cap flew into the caged partition, and he grabbed it and stuffed it deeper into the bag. He wouldn't need it again tonight.

Easter Sunday morning demanded his attention, and he had hoped to get out a little early in order to catch two or three hours of sleep before the sunrise service at the church.

His most important assignment of the day would be removing the bags of candy from the trunk of his wife's car and furtively secreting plastic eggs all over the backyard before the kids woke up. He determined that he would probably miss the sunrise service since he was going to get into bed just as the sun began streaming through the bedroom window. Maybe he would just meet the family at the 10:30 service—this night had kicked him in his fuzzy little tail.

He had a power shower in the locker room before throwing on his jeans and a sweatshirt. His Old Spice deodorant was just about gone, but he was able to remove enough of the blue gel-like remnants to get a little under each arm and more than he wanted on his hands. He chucked the empty canister into the metal trash can beside the sink and jogged out the back door of the building to get into his pickup truck.

He rolled the windows down to help him remain wide awake. Between the new Old Dominion downloads Bluetooth'd to his stereo and the cold breeze shooting through his wet hair, there was no way he would doze off on the ride home.

He turned up the gravel driveway and braced himself for the familiar jolts to the Chevy's aging suspension. April downpours and poor drainage had turned his driveway into a rocky obstacle course with no escape paths. He powered through, turned out the lights, and parked on the grass some distance from the house in order to avoid waking the kids when he shut the door of the truck.

The bags of candy were right where she said they would be. A box of multi-colored plastic two-piece egg shells were there too. He had stuffed a whole Cadbury egg into his mouth when he heard her shuffling slippers coming across the dooryard. He turned his flashlight toward her to blind her from seeing the sugary yolk-like substance running down from corner of his mouth, but it was too late.

"How many have you had?" she inquired. He tried to say,

"Just one," but his retort was bathed in the rich chocolate and subsequent creamy center. It sounded more like "Jaarrghh un." She knew what he meant, and she laughed at him exactly like he expected.

Together they filled the eggs with jelly beans and tiny chocolate eggs. There were six more Cadbury cream eggs too, and all of them made it to slightly visible spots in the backyard, near the shed, and on top of the gas grill.

As they walked back to the house, she mentioned that he smelled like he had been preening for a date. He explained his dilemma with the last of the deodorant and wondered, out loud, if she felt more attracted to him. She said, "Not at all. You need to go to bed. I'll take Dory and Sam to Sunday school and you can meet us for the 10:30 service. We are going to your parent's house for dinner after the service."

He grunted and threw his clothes on the floor as he dove into the cool sheets. He had done his rabbit-ly duties, and he dozed into a slumber quickly. His dream about moving remarkably light boulders into the bed of an old Dodge Power Wagon was interrupted by Dory and Samuel rooting around in the backyard, discovering what the "Bunny" had left behind. Dreams don't always make sense, but the sound of children being childish made perfect sense.

It became a numbers game, and Sam was already hollering to his mother that Dory had found more than her fair share. He smiled as the sun streamed through the window directly into his face.

His phone woke him what seemed like only moments later. He threw on his blue suit, white shirt, and yellow necktie. He flicked a little water on his hair again and ran his wife's brush through the remnants of what was once a marvelous head of hair. The brush was barely slowed by his college cut, and it was futile trying to tame such a small flock of locks; the short hair on the crown of his head always had alternate travel plans.

He came into the service during the last hymn before the sermon and tried to slide into the row of seats as quietly as possible, but, as usual, he kicked the steel leg of the chair in front of him, and the clang was amplified by a quiet moment just before the song ended.

He'd cut it close, but he'd made it.

Dory climbed into his lap for her neck-hug and subsequent sweet-voiced mention about his beard being rough. She leaned in close and whispered, "Daddy, I think the Easter Bunny wears the same deodorant as you do." He tried to create a surprised look with his tired eyes and recoiled his head back to add to the effect.

The six-year-old looked at him earnestly and explained that all of the plastic eggs in the backyard smelled exactly like he did. He smiled and whispered, "The Easter Bunny has really good taste in men's fragrances. Did he bring you any Cadbury eggs?"

Dory smiled and shook her head up and down and added, "Mommy said you like them, too, so I saved you one." He hugged her close and reached over to give Sam a loving pre-sermon father-to-son noogie. Sam looked up and revealed a wide grin framed by just the right amount of chocolate.

He settled into the uncomfortable seat, surrounded by everything he needed and nothing he didn't. He wished he had put some jelly beans in his pocket but figured he could scam a few from Sam around mid-service.

Boots

The steel door to the locker room needed a coat of paint. All of the doors in the station had a strip of scrapes and chips about forty inches from the bottom. A sure sign that many police officers had walked in and out over the years.

A Sam Brown belt with a gun and a portable radio on opposing sides was the perfect "third hand" for holding open the door while trying to balance a duty bag, coats, hats, and whatever else needed to be carried in and out of the station.

The locker room door was battleship-steel color but built from thinner material, of course. If he looked closely, he could see previous coats of paint showing through the worn top layer. There was really no purpose in looking that closely; the other coats were also gray.

The paint was probably purchased in bulk sometime in the '60s, when gray steel desks and filing cabinets were the office chic of recycled government-issue furniture from the military base in town. Many of those desks and filing cabinets were still being utilized. The filing cabinet drawers still rolled on ball bearings made to last until the gray paint wore off. There was no worry of that as there apparently were plenty of spare cabinets.

He pushed the door open with his hip, as his uniforms were in his right hand, hung on wire hangers from home. He liked wire hangers, even though Betty Davis did not. They could be used for many purposes if fashioned correctly. He had used a wire coat hanger to pull the keys out of the center console of a Tahoe a few weeks ago. The window was left open about a half inch, which is not enough room to pull a set of keys through. It was, however, a large enough crack to push his silver Cross pen through in order to poke the unlock button on the key fob. He asked the woman if she was a school custodian. She didn't get the joke but brought him oatmeal raisin cookies the next day. A wire coat hanger can make cookies appear. Try that with a wooden coat hanger.

The shower steam carried with it the odor of body wash with just a hint of coconut, possibly some mango—likely one of the rookies, probably using a pouf. He saw the fashionable Nike flip flops below the curtain. Whoever it was had a Daytona Beach towel slung over the shower curtain rod. Florida would be nice right now; it was spring in Bangor, but it was thirty-four degrees. He might take his light jacket tonight.

He headed down the narrow aisle between the lockers. Who designed this locker room? Every time he walked through, it felt narrower. Frodo would be happy here; maybe Frodo was in the shower. He laughed at the vision of Frodo on Daytona Beach wearing flip-flops, smelling of coconut with a hint of mango. He knew Frodo did not roll like that. He probably smelled more like the Old Forest, which would be a great name for a body wash. Note to self: send that idea to Old Spice for a new deodorant moniker.

He saw his boots on top of his locker. He never looked at the number on the door, and there were times he forgot it altogether.

He knew his boots, though. He placed them on top of the old green locker before he went home after each shift. He kept them polished, within reason. He put his uniforms inside the locker—a locker that did not smell like boots for the obvious reason. Most everyone kept their working boots on top. If you were creative with a little duct tape and a wooden block, you could store your spare boots there as well.

Dress boots for special occasions were kept inside the locker. He didn't like wearing his dress boots, because wearing them meant that a current officer or retiree had passed away. He could never wear his day-to-day boots to a funeral. It would show zero respect to those who had gone on before the rest. Their family and friends deserved to see gleaming toes and pressed dark-blue uniforms. It was the least he could do.

He flicked open the Pandora app on his scratched and gouged iPhone 5C—the cheap white one. It worked well enough. His son had picked up an iPhone 7 or 10, or whatever, and he now had his son's old phone. Pandora was already installed, and he determined that he liked being able to pick his kind of music. Pablo Cruise came up first, and it made getting dressed seem like a '70s proposition. It made him smile.

Well everybody's heart needs a holiday, some time
And every one of us needs to get away, some how
'Cause laughing light-hearted moods
Oh, sight-seeing afternoons
And telling a joke or two
'Cause everyday invites you to find your place in the sun
It's time to find your place in the sun
Find your place
Find your place in the sun
It's time to find your place in the sun.

Frodo walked behind him wrapped in his Daytona Beach towel. The song seemed to fit. Frodo didn't think so. He asked the name of the band.

Being bent over to pull on his right boot caused his answer to sound labored, "Pablo Cruise."

"Wasn't that the name of a drug lord or something?" Frodo inquired.

He sat up and said, "No, that was Pablo Escobar. He wasn't known for singing upbeat '70's party music. He was murdering people and selling tons of cocaine. He might have listened to Pablo Cruise. I have my doubts, but I am, and right now you are talking over the best part."

Frodo disappeared behind the next line of lockers, dripping water and humming unknowingly to the music (to which he had most recently been introduced).

He picked up his left boot and looked at the cracks in the leather and dried mud in the welt around the worn sole. It came from a mud puddle in a driveway on French Street. He had arrested a man there on his last shift two nights ago. He had tried to avoid the puddle, but the man led him right through it when he tried to break free. The man didn't get far, but he had to give him credit for trying. He wasn't fighting, just trying to run. Better to have muddy boots than a bloody lip or worse.

The boots needed a polish, maybe a new Vibram sole. They would last another six months until the yearly boot allowance was given out. He would opt to re-sole them if possible. They were expensive boots, and they were more expensive now, even when ordered through the police supply company. He liked the way they felt on his feet. The right boot squeaked from time to time. How does that happen? A boot with a squeak. It came and went intermittently, like the squeak on his Ford pickup. He had learned to press his toes down harder when it happened to make it stop squeaking—not the truck, the boot.

He threw the phone on top of his gear bag as he walked toward the gray door. He liked the idea of walking out to his cruiser with a soundtrack. What would Pandora give him tonight? The Doobie Brothers' "Nobody" came on. One of his favorite songs from one of his favorite bands. He squeezed by Frodo, who was now dressed and looking sharp in his Class Bs. He still smelled like mango, though.

Frodo said, "Hey, your boot creaks when you walk."

He walked toward the battleship gray door and mumbled, "So do I, Frodo, so do I."

The Marine

The night air felt good on his face. Spring was slow to become summer, the way it always does—warm days and cold nights. The dash vent, appropriately aimed, allowed a stream of warm air to hit him near his left shoulder while the driver's side window was retracted down, inside the door.

The cool breeze brought in the smells of spring in Maine pine, cedar, and the residue of the residents at Young's dairy farm.

He was alone after 0200. His sergeant and another patrol officer passed him outbound on Western Avenue at about 0205. Bumper to bumper, the two now-off-duty officers wasted no time heading home after their shift. Of course they knew where he was parked while he had been running radar. He was positive they enjoyed the thought of him hearing the radar tones scream when their cars came over the rise at twenty over the posted limit. He had done it, as well. It's good for a laugh the first time.

It was funnier the day the sergeant received a handwritten note in his work mailbox; it was signed by the town manager. According to the message, a resident, walking his dog, had seen him

251

speeding out of the lot in his personal vehicle around 0203. "The man" had called the town manager to complain.

The sergeant went in and admitted to his hasty departure even before a pleasant salutation from the town's boss. When she told him she had no idea what he was talking about, he knew he had been duped by someone who was sick of hearing the radar scream at 0205. All is fair in love and war.

For the next four hours, the town would be his oyster. The end of shift came at 0600 and that would be the pearl he focused on.

The dark blue Caprice had four speakers connected to the FM radio. Chevrolet's fleet division must have hired a genius who understood that a single speaker in the middle of the dashboard would not reproduce "Blackwater" by The Doobie Brothers the way it was intended to be heard. He sang along only after making sure his knee would not key-up the transmit button on the microphone. The technician who located the mic holder that low on the dash was trying to get him in trouble. He took the mic and hung it over the rearview mirror like a trucker. This would guarantee his singing was kept within the confines of the Chevy. It was good for him; good for America.

At 0323 he stopped a young male driving an older Nissan pickup truck. The one headlamp that was operable was flickering like a neon sign at a desert roadhouse. The operator was polite but very nervous. The cop found out why when he ran his name through the dispatcher.

"303, are you 10-15?" He knew the question well. She was asking him if he was within earshot of the driver, which probably meant the young lad had a suspended driver's license or an active warrant for his arrest. He told dispatch that he was not 10-15, and she confirmed the warrant. It was for the kid's failure to pay a fine. A lousy twenty-five dollars was the difference between freedom and jail for the night.

The kid was pleasant, and the cop hoped the boy had the money to pay his fine and then be on his way again in the old Nissan with the flickering headlamp. The cop asked if he had the money to pay as he placed him in handcuffs and searched him for weapons. There were no weapons, of course, but he didn't have the twenty-five bucks either.

The cop felt bad but also had to fulfill his obligation to the system. The young man was twenty-one and had been working and paying off his fine for a minor criminal mischief charge on the court-ordered payment plan. As they drove toward the jail, the man told the cop that he had been out with friends for a couple of beers before he headed out of town in the morning. He said he had signed up for the Marine Corps and had to be in the recruiter's office by 1300 that day. The recruiter was going to put him on the bus with a final destination of Parris Island, South Carolina.

The cop asked the man if he had any proof of being signed up to leave for boot camp. The muffled voice from the backseat explained that his paperwork was over the visor in the Nissan they had left behind in the grocery store parking lot. The cop did a quick three-point turn and headed back to the truck. When they pulled up, he grabbed his flashlight and instinctively told the kid to stay put. Of course, the kid had no choice. The cop found the orders and documents that verified the story.

He told the kid that he would need to see the judge at 0830 and that he needed to pay his fine to get things squared away. The kid remained respectful, calling him "sir" way too much, and reiterated he did not have the twenty-five dollars; he had only had seven dollars and some change.

Once inside the jail, the cop did the paperwork, verified the amount that would take care of the fine, and then walked over to the kid in the chair waiting to be booked in for the lousy charge. He inquired if he would be able to make a few phone calls to raise the money from his folks or a friend. The boy said his folks loaned him the money to go out tonight with his buddies. They had nothing extra and were not in a good financial situation. His friends would never be able to come up with the money.

"I am going to loan you the money to get this taken care of," the cop said quietly. "You are going to be on that bus this afternoon to Parris Island. I will meet you in the lobby of the courthouse at 0830 when they bring you over. You can then see the judge, pay the clerk, and get yourself something to eat before hoofing it over to the recruiter's office on Harlow Street." The kid seemed surprised and pleased. He just shook his head up and down and settled into his chair.

The cop backed the Chevy out of the sally port and headed to the ATM nearby. He inserted his card, punched in the code, and took out four crisp ten-dollar bills. He slipped them in his pocket and headed back to town to finish out his shift.

He got off at 0600, changed his clothes, and grabbed a bite to eat at his favorite breakfast spot. At 0830, the cop walked into the courthouse and found the young man sitting on the bench near the clerk's office. He was waiting for his first appearance in front of the judge.

The cop looked at him and told him clearly that it was a loan but that it was important he made the bus to boot camp. The young man thanked him, called him sir, and promised to pay the money back when he could.

The cop slipped the four crisp ten-dollar bills into the boy's shirt pocket, wished him good luck, and said that he should have at least five dollars left over after his fines and fees were paid. He advised he should grab a burger when he walked out of the court-house and that the meal was a gift. The rest of the money was a loan. The boy thanked him again, and the cop walked out the courthouse doors. He needed to go to bed.

The cop called the recruiter's office the following day and confirmed the boy had made it to the bus. He knew the toughest part of the adventure, and hopefully a career, were ahead of the young man. He would probably need to work a couple of overtime shifts in the next couple of weeks to replenish his reserve account. He did not expect to get his money back, but he considered it an investment in his own future. The kid would probably become a great Marine.

The Canoe

Pete, the Quik-Pik clerk, saw him pulling in at 0237 and rushed across the store to the four-pot Bunn coffee machine in order to make a fresh pot.

Similar stainless sentinels stand watch in small stores all over America. With a little coaxing from Pete, it made the best coffee in town. Incidentally, it was the only coffee in town at that hour. Pete made sure the machine was clean and that the pots were always spotless. He worked six nights a week, didn't talk much about his past life as a bookkeeper, and always said, "God rest her soul," when he spoke of his wife.

The widower's boat shoes had come apart about five years before. The smooth and formerly flapping soles were held to the blotched-brown leather uppers by several frayed loops of four-and-a-half-year-old silver duct tape. The stuff held nicely. Pete claimed the shoes were better than new.

What should have been a signature squeak of synthetic rubber soles on the well-waxed, but aging, tan-colored tile floors had now taken on the tones of a fine pair of footie pajamas being shushed across a kitchen floor by a four-year-old searching for a morning bowl of Rice Krispies. Shush, shush, shush, scuff, shush.

"Don't grab it yet. I just started it when you pulled in."

The cop walked over to the magazine rack and perused a swap-and-sell guide for a few minutes. He needed to find a new-to-him, reasonably priced canoe. His old Grumman sixteen-footer had been run over by a pickup truck at a tent site near Big Pleasant Pond just a few weeks before.

"Still looking for a canoe?" Pete asked, wearing his signature smirk.

"Yes, Pete, I am still looking for a canoe," came the reply from behind the racks of Bic lighters, cheap mirrored sunglasses, and corn chips.

"You shouldn't have run over your last one!"

"I never should have told you that story, and let's be clear, I *backed* over it," the cop replied defensively as he put the magazine back on the rickety wire rack.

"There will be a time when you can let that go, and we can start our conversations with things like, I hope your night has been fabulous, and, Good to see you."

Pete laughed again and pulled the Winston cigarette out from behind his ear. "You gonna be here a minute?" he asked as he stepped outside. He kept the door open to listen for the phone, which never rang after midnight.

The cop said, "I have to wait for the last bit of nectar to drip into that pot, don't I?"

Pete used a paper match to light the cancer stick and took a drag. He held the smoke in his lungs like he had taken an oath to keep it safe from all harm, only freeing it to the cold night air when he determined he needed to make room for another.

The sulfur from the match hung in the air for a moment, and the cop caught a whiff. For some reason, the smell of burned paper matches and freshly lit tobacco carried memories of fishing trips with his buddies who smoked as they sat quietly with rod in one hand, butt in the other, patiently overlooking brooks and small ponds around Maine.

The cop had never smoked. His grandmother had died of complications from a stroke, brought on, in part, from cigarette smoking. It never seemed like a good idea.

He watched Pete smoke like a poorly shod movie star as he looked up at the stars and hummed unnamed songs. Pete waved at a couple of regularly scheduled truckers who passed at speed; honking the air horns as they rattled their overloaded diesels up the hill near the store.

Six nights a week, Pete was the unelected mayor of that dark stretch of lonely road. A welcome conversationalist for the lonely ladies leaving the late shift, a cheerful cheerleader for scratch-off addicts who thought they were winning because they collected five dollars in proceeds after buying ten dollars' worth of tickets, and all the men who needed a cold sixer placed in a crisp paper bag, which had to be snapped to attention by the widowed clerk who had held far better jobs but treated this one like it was the best job he ever had.

Pete walked back in and poured two cups of coffee, one for the cop and one for himself. His vintage aviator glasses were bent, and had apparently been bent back, in several crooked spots along the temple. His green Izod golf shirt, untucked, was faded but clean. He wore Levi's that always showed a well-ironed crease.

From a distance, he looked like a neatly dressed older man going to a minor league baseball game in late summer. Up close, and over a deeply-discounted cup of early morning coffee, he looked like a worn-down and smiling widower who enjoyed the company of a diverse group of people with similar stories.

Pete growled, "Arrest anyone tonight?"

The cop replied, "Not yet, unless you have a sordid criminal past that you have been keeping from me."

Pete smiled and asked if the coffee was at least adequate.

The cop said, "Barely."

They both laughed and sipped as the hum of the cooler compressors filled in the moments of silence between the two tired men conversing about nothing in particular.

Pete said, "Walk out back with me."

The cop asked if he treated all his customers this way.

Pete replied, "Only the customers who can't back up a pickup truck while camping fifty miles from the nearest asphalt."

They meandered through the storeroom, stepping over cases of candy bars, paper products, and flats of Diet Coke and root beer. Pete unlocked the steel door after disarming the panic-bar alarm and opened it into alley where he parked his rusty 1988 Ford Ranger.

The roof rack on the aluminum truck cap held a red, scratched and dinged, Old Town Royalex Tripper canoe. He asked the cop if it looked familiar.

"Nope, it doesn't."

The cop's answer made Pete's night all the better as it allowed him to deliver a line that sounded like it had been practiced for days. "That's because it's not flat on one end like the one you destroyed on your camping trip!"

Pete laughed; the cop smiled and replied, "Well, which river are you going to? The St. John? Allagash? St. Croix?"

Pete said, "Where do *you* want to go? It's yours now. I haven't used it since 1983. My wife and I used to fish the Union River in that boat. Haven't put it in the water since she died, God rest her soul."

"I can't take your boat, Pete. Let me buy it from you. That boat is worth 750 bucks at a minimum. I'll get you the money next week."

Pete scowled and said, "I don't want your money. I want this thing out of my barn. Take it. When you have a son or a daughter, tell them Uncle Peter wanted them to go fishing. I'll drop it in your yard on the way home from the store in the morning. I'll put it out in back of your place, on the grass. Don't run it over."

They finished their coffee outside, in front of the store, while Pete had another smoke. The cop said, "Pete, is there anything you need that I could trade you for the boat? It's so kind of you to offer, but I don't feel right about taking it for nothing."

Pete scowled and said, "I have to get back to work. The boat will be in your dooryard tomorrow. That's the end of the story. Go camping again when you get some time off. It paddles well and is a lot more stable than your old Grumman, especially now that it's flat on one end. You will never make your twenty-five years if you don't take some time for yourself." Pete blew Winston smoke up into the air like he was crop dusting the stars "Buy me a roll of duct tape so I can polish my shoes."

"I'll do that Pete; I'll do that. They even make the stuff in brown now."

He flashed his spotlight through the window as he drove up the hill toward his remaining business checks. Pete flipped him the bird. Pete was kind like that.

The Widow

He sat with the widow for over half an hour before she spoke. "We went to breakfast today, everything seemed fine." He just nodded his head to indicate that he'd heard what she said. He knew that his words were unnecessary and useless; he kept them to himself. Silence is difficult for some people; he embraced it knowing it was exactly what she needed.

He picked up the yellow plastic tumbler of water from the coffee table and took a sip. He wasn't even thirsty, but it seemed like a good way to act comfortable for her. One of the toughest things to learn as a cop is to be what someone needs you to be at that very moment. This was a perfect moment to be quiet and just be there. He wanted her to know he appreciated the water. She noticed and asked if he needed any more. He told her he was fine and offered her the same. She told him that she wouldn't say no to a cup of tea.

He went to the kitchen, which was directly under the second floor bedroom where her husband had shot himself less than two hours ago. He could hear the evidence technicians as they worked to determine whether the gunshot had been self-inflicted. He trusted their expertise. He had worked with them for years. They were good at what they did. As morbid and horrific as the job could be, they worked through it like they were old carpenters determining where to put the new porch. You just knew it would be right when they were done.

The porcelain coating on the white gas stove was chipped but perfectly clean. The Revere-Ware teapot had a cracked plastic stopper but the whistle still worked. The trigger to open the stopper worked reliably. He had seen a lot of teapots, and this looked like all the others. It seemed that someone should be able to come up with a better material for a stopper. As he could recall, the only one he had ever seen intact was the one he'd bought for his mother a few years before she passed away. He had it on his stove now. He rarely made tea, but he did secretly enjoy a mug of Swiss Miss instant cocoa.

He carried the mug of tea and placed it on the stained end table beside her chair. She said nothing. He was glad. He sat back down and looked over his notes regarding what she had told him earlier when she was talking and crying. He hoped her daughter would arrive soon. He wouldn't leave until the removal of her husband, but he crossed his fingers that her daughter would get there to give her the support she needed for the rest of the day.

She looked up and thanked him for the tea. He said she was very welcome and that he would be willing to call some other folks if she wanted him to. She said that she would wait for her daughter. He understood and pretended to look through the email on his phone.

She asked him if he was married, and he told her that he used to be. She apologized for prying but he told her that he was glad to talk to her about it. She asked if he had children, and he said he had two, one in college and one in the Marines. She said that he must be proud. He said that he was.

Then they were silent again—probably the kind of silence that she never expected on a Saturday in winter; not this winter anyway.

She said he had been bothered with dire finances, his lack of work, and his depression. Today he had seemed happy to go out for a meal with her. She said she felt more positive about things. They were getting by.

She blurted out, "Do you see this much?" He answered that he saw it more frequently than he liked and that he hoped she would call her pastor or a close friend. She promised that she would, but only after she talked to her daughter. He said, "I completely understand." She asked him if it was quick. He said it was. She seemed relieved and sipped her tea.

The questions witnesses and victims ask after traumatic incidents are not what people expect them to be. Television has created millions of experts in field investigations. However, most of the millions do not realize they were trained by actors—actually, writers who were not even actors. No questions surprised him, and hers were on-point and exactly what he expected. He did not watch crime dramas. He did like *Barney Miller*.

The cop excused himself and went upstairs to check on the techs. They were almost done. There was no doubt that the man had done this purposefully. The note was clear. She had found it when she found him. It made his stomach turn to know she had discovered all this, and then a note. His scribbling indicated that he loved her and felt she would do better without him. It was a permanent solution to a temporary problem.

To the husband, it had felt permanent, and he did not want that anymore. He had purchased insurance quite a while ago. Contrary to the public forums, taking one's own life through suicide does not always preclude payment. He had planned this well. A good man with an aching soul. So many were out there. Most are quiet about it.

The woman's daughter arrived and the cop made sure to stand by for any questions he could answer. It was uncomfortable all over again, maybe more so.

When the attendants from the funeral home arrived, they handled it perfectly. He had much respect for the way they dressed in gray suits and muted ties. A recent widow deserves to see things handled in a manner that indicates her husband was important, mainly because he was important.

Many people only see the end result at a beautifully orchestrated funeral. The real work was done during a removal. The real respect was shown by men and women the victim would never meet. They even parked in a location that was respectful and would not draw inquiries from the neighbors.

The cop knew them from many late-night meetings not at all unlike this one. He shared with them the names of the wife and the daughter so they could use their names when speaking to them about the plans. It set a tone and indicated to the loved ones that the men in the dark jackets cared, as well. The cop knew they did. No one did this kind of work because it was exciting and glamorous. Their well-pressed suits appeared expensive, but their shoes had just carried them through late February mud. There was a story there. Someday he thought he might write it.

Hugs were exchanged between the widow and all the cops. She wanted to thank them for whatever they did to make the worst day of her life a little better. Larry called her "dear," and he meant it. Who said an evidence tech is not intuitive?

He passed her his card and explained how a post-mortem examination would be carried out. It was just to be sure that the story the evidence told was completely accurate—checks and balances. She did not want to hear about it, but she listened because she knew that she needed to know. Her daughter rubbed her shoulders.

Three weeks later, the widow sent a note. It just read, "Thank you." He tucked it into his bottom desk drawer with a few others. He grabbed his coat and yelled across the cube farm to find out who was buying lunch today. Larry's voice replied, "Not me, but I'll drive." He yelled back, "Of course you will; it's city gas." He slammed the drawer shut and decided that he would buy today. Larry had called her "dear" at just the right time. One word, on one bad day, yet so important to the widow who might never hear that word again.

Leaning on the Sill

He was tired—tired because he hadn't been sleeping that well in the heat of the summer days, tired of trying to figure out how to make each paycheck stretch to the next one, and tired of being grouchy with his wife just before he left for work at 7:45 P.M. Shift work has its benefits; he just couldn't think of one right now.

She still hugged him like she always did. They had agreed early on that an argument should not trump a hug, or a kiss, or a wink. Even on "fight nights," as he liked to refer to it, he would pull into the driveway sometime during the eleven o'clock news. Inevitably it would be during the weather portion of the local newscast. He felt the forecast should last about three minutes, but it seemed like it lasted for about twenty-four of the twenty-six minutes of actual programming.

The summer routine was that he would pull into the driveway, flash his headlights, and she would scoot over toward the screen near her end of the couch. He would lean on the elbow-worn outer sill and tell her he was sorry, or that he forgot to tell her something earlier that day. He could have gone inside, but this was the summer routine. It was bizarre to some, but they both liked the throwback to simpler times—the times before babies and bills, shift work and scraping by.

He used to do the same thing when they were dating, back when she was finishing college while living at her mom's house. The worn path to the wood line should have been a giveaway to late-night screen-talks, but her mother never mentioned it— well, not until about a year after they were married, when Sybil (only he called her Sybil—her name was Martha) mentioned that she never had to trim the grass around her daughter's window in years past but that the grass was growing "wonderfully now." She'd winked at him.

Now their screen-talks only lasted about five to ten minutes, she would tell him to go save some lives; he would tell her to sleep well and that she should keep in mind that he only works after dark because, "Everyone knows that's where evil lurks." She would shut the window and blow him a kiss.

About once a summer, sometimes twice, he would return to the window to talk to her again— usually after a particularly bad call, or maybe a death, a fight, or even a death notification.

When that happened, he would flash his spotlight through their left bedroom window. A couple of flashes off the mirror on the far wall would bring her around. It didn't wake the kids like a phone ringing. It didn't cause the dog to bark like his footsteps would if he was clunking across the back porch. She would come down and slide up the glass and ask him how he was. He would tell her.

Inevitably he would thank her for her time, ask her how much for the session. He would tell her that it should only be five cents, like Lucy used to charge Charlie Brown.

She reminded him of Lucy when she leaned on the window-sill and just listened. They would joke that he did not have a nick-el today, but that she could send a bill to the department. She said she would just keep his football until he could come up with the cash. They would laugh at the stupidity of comparing their lives to *Peanuts*, but that's what you do. You sometimes need to laugh.

The truth of the matter was that he didn't have even a nickel in his pocket, but he had her. On those nights—and many others—it was more than enough.

The Voice

The baby woke her up at 12:10 A.M.—12-10 was also her anniversary. She was married to the man who lay snoozing with one foot hanging over the edge of the bed. His unclothed calves shone brightly in the dim light of the green-hued digital clock radio. He needed some sun, but this is Maine in the winter. He would get no sun, so she covered him up.

She wished he would buy new pajamas. No one needs to see all that at 12:10 A.M.

The good and the bad news was that she needed to be in the communications center at 0300 to pay back her co-worker for taking her December 10 shift so she could have the night off to go to dinner with Mr. Snoozy. Dinner was good. Payback was a b$*#@.

He never wakes up when the baby cries. Or does he? He certainly would make a great sloth, possibly a possum. He could play dead with the best of them. He worked shift work too. He was finally on evenings after fourteen years. He deserved it. She let him sleep.

The baby stopped crying the minute she picked him up and spoke to him—a bottle, diaper, a belch, and her work was completed.

The next time he cried, her husband would have to get up. She wouldn't be there anyway. She would be answering the phone at the police department. Oh, the joy and glamour of the shift-working mother. She loved her job as a dispatcher, but it was brutal on her internal clock—much worse since the baby was born.

The dispatch center was quiet. She would take the fire department tonight. They all swapped off, one night dispatching fire and EMS, one night the police. She was hoping for no calls. She only had to work until 10 A.M. to pay Jimmy back for the night off. It was good of him to work for her.

Vacation days were hard to get since they had been running short-staffed. Everyone pulled their weight. Jimmy pulled more than his weight. They were all close in the com center. You had to be close as you spent more time with them than with your own family.

Holidays were like any other day, except someone would bring in leftovers for them to feel like they were having a real Thanksgiving or Christmas meal—not the same, but not bad. She wished for wine, all she got was whine. Complainants can be needy and a little pushy.

Her first call was for the transport of an eighty-four-year-old woman with severe chest pain. The patient's husband had called before, and, if his wife continued on this path, he would need their help again.

The man was so sweet on the phone. He recognized the dispatcher's voice. He calmed considerably when she told him that the paramedics would be there in less than three minutes.

He told her he would turn the porch light on. She was happy he remembered. Her tone made him feel somehow better. She remembered his name, and he felt like he had a friend. It was a typical call for her, but for the man, she was an angel.

Tonight his wife would be fine.

The old man would speak to the dispatcher again in a few weeks when his wife passed away suddenly in the night. He didn't know that yet, but her voice would make the difference.

The voice that calmed the baby was the same voice that would make the death of his wife more tolerable. Horrific, but better.

That's why she does this.

Thank you to our dispatchers who do one of the most thankless jobs in public safety. I couldn't do your job for even a moment. We all appreciate you. I am not sending flowers, all I have are words. They will never be enough.

.

Afterword—The Story of Phil Winslow

If there was a turning point in the way we presented the Bangor Maine Police Department on Facebook, I would say it occurred in June of 2014. I had taken to the keyboard more, writing excessively wordy posts and using very few pictures. I didn't have any photos to share. That changed as time went on, and I pummeled my co-workers with requests to send me photos at any time of the day or night.

I told the willing participants in my trek through the wilderness of social media that if they shared with me just a couple of details pertaining to the photos they provided, that I would write something, anything, to try to make it fun and interesting for the people who read about us on the book of faces.

When I didn't get any photos, I'd wake up and wing it. I found, on some days, that just typing many sentences directly into the computer would help me come up with something to share. After writing a story or an anecdote, I would scratch around in the dusty recesses of my mind for a way to relate it to police work. I could usually do it, but at times it was a stretch.

The fact of the matter is, I cannot reiterate to you how little I understood about why it was working.

The good news is that there really wasn't any pressure—from anyone—to perform. When you have no idea what you are doing, you can find some comfort in the fact that other people don't know what you should be doing.

There was no one in the building who wanted to tell our story on social media. It was a fly-by-night, seat-of-the pants experiment, and, since I was in charge, I did the only thing I knew how to do. I got out of bed each morning—I had that part figured out—and I wrote stuff.

Feel free to steal my secret.

I wake up early every day; I have no control over that. I just can't sleep much longer than five hours. I would write the posts on my couch, right after I fed the dog, took her out, and made coffee; then I would sit down to inject words into the MacBook.

Of course, I wanted it to be related to the mission of our agency, but I also wanted to be relatable to those who took the time to click over and see what we were doing. I had no intention of creating a national audience for our page. It wasn't even on my radar. It just happened. I'm pleased that it did, but when I started getting phone calls from people asking me what my secret was, I had to tell them the truth.

"I just write stuff that makes me smile; then I hit 'publish.'" It's really easy to do.

I received some commentary from individuals who fancied themselves social media professionals; all of them agreed that what I was doing wouldn't work on Facebook. I was somewhat confused, as you can imagine. I asked them what they thought would work better, or at least what might work well.

Their answers were mostly centered on the fact that I was being too "wordy," and I wasn't sharing enough photos. I decided to continue doing the same thing, at least until it stopped working so well. But it didn't stop working.

I had been tossed the keys to the Facebook page in mid-May, and, by June, we had doubled our original audience from 9,000 followers, to somewhere just south of 20,000. We never paid to promote a post. Every "like," "comment," and "share" was an organic event.

I didn't even know you could pay to have a post promoted until about a year into this mess. Still, we never paid; we had no budget. I did not know what I was doing, yet people from around the world were reading about Bangor, Maine's police department.

Just before Independence Day in 2014, I determined that I would write something humorous to spread the message that the City of Bangor did not allow explosive-type fireworks to be detonated inside city limits. It was just a public service announcement written in a campy and sarcastic tone.

Someone from National Public Radio read the piece, and one of their producers called and asked if I would be willing to narrate the missive for their nationally broadcast *Morning Edition* on the Fourth of July in 2014.

I agreed to do it, just because I thought it would be rather funny. The producers added some patriotic music in the background, and it was featured during the broadcast.

We saw a huge uptick in followers that week, and things really started to roll along as we began to gather readers from all over the world.

A couple of weeks later, on a hot Sunday afternoon, my wife and I were riding back from our little cabin in far Down East Maine. I stopped to help an elderly man whose car had broken down on the side of the road. His name was Phil Winslow, and the interaction turned into quite an event. Since my wife had taken a photo of Phil and me while I worked and Phil talked, I decided to tell the story of people coming together in the Maine woods.

This was the first time that I wrote about a non-police-related event for our page. The reactions were so positive from around the world that I was somewhat shocked. It was just a simple story, but it struck a chord with so many people.

The post comes up in my Facebook feed every year around the twentieth of July. To date, it has been viewed at least a million times, and it is shared and re-shared on a pretty regular basis.

I wrote the piece late that evening at my home. The writing was actually pretty horrible. I pecked it out on the tiny keyboard on my phone and added the photo that my wife had taken. Within a few days, I realized that people were looking for more stories just like this one.

It was merely a simple tale of folks helping other folks. I knew then that I was going to continue to just go with my instincts and share stories about humans and their interactions with the people around them. For the first time, I had a plan.

From that point on, I paid no mind to any commonly followed rules of social media. I stopped being worried about writing pieces that were too long. My gut instinct was that people would read, and enjoy, stories that made them feel good.

I decided to include this story exactly how it was written for the page. You can get a feel for the sometimes-bizarre way I construct sentences. After this came out, I started to receive inquiries about whether we had hired a professional social media manager.

I just told people that it was only me, and I was just "writing stuff." Here is the story of Phil Winslow and his flat tire.

We get jaded. All of us. Today, I had a great experience and I am sharing it. Maybe because it makes me feel less jaded and might make you feel the same way as well.

My lovely wife and I were traveling back from a weekend with my son and his "lady-friend." As we were traveling Route 182 we saw a gentleman wheeling his Oldsmobile to the side of the road and it appeared he had a flat. It was hot.

My wife, who works with seniors, immediately noticed that the man was not young and pointed that out to me. He had come to a stop in a bad spot, at least for changing a tire.

If you are from Maine, you know there are no real great spots to change a tire. Paved shoulders are rare and we all know you don't get a flat anywhere near a paved shoulder. I pulled up and got out. The gentleman had a catastrophic flat. Gone, baby, gone. He was pretty happy we stopped and I told him that I could easily do this for him.

He was on his way from Belfast, where he'd seen his kids, and driving home to Mapleton. I thought to myself, you really shouldn't get there from here, but I am from Maine and know anything is possible if you have a *Gazetteer* and a sense of adventure.

My wife took a photo of Phillip Winslow and me. It was his 85th birthday.

All of the sudden it wasn't so hot outside and what a great guy he was to talk to. We found his spare and all the tools and set to work.

Cars whizzed by over the hill in the background and they did not slow nor move over. I was concerned and asked Phil to at least move to the side of the car near the woods but he wanted to help. He told me that last year he could almost leap up and down and over the past year, the leaping has stopped and he has a more difficult time getting around.

I realized shortly that the wheel was "rust-welded" to the rotor and I was not in my truck and thus not carrying my tools (big hammers are a must for these occasions). That's when the lovely and talented Lois stopped. She lived nearby and had a selection of hammers. I asked for a big one and she said she would run to the house and grab a couple. She was the kind of lady that you want to meet when changing a tire.

She came right back with two optimum sized hammers and I set to work on banging the wheel off. Perfect, I said, this will be easy. Then after returning the hammers to Lois, she left and came back with three waters and an offer for a bathroom.

Now, I had met Phil, who I liked very much, and Lois, who was becoming my new favorite person. She dropped the water off to us and offered a cool place for Phil to sit if he needed it. He said "No," as he likes to help. She left, but said she was just up the road if we needed any more help.

As we continued, the sand gave out from under the jack. The car fell onto the shoulder of the road. Not good. Phil and I laughed a little and then Phil got in our car with the wife to cool off. I called AAA for a good jack and we all waited together.

While waiting, a lovely lady stopped in a newer Hyundai and said she had a floor jack in her car. You have to love Maine women—hammers and floor jacks. I told her Triple A was coming and soon they did. All was well.

We got Phil headed to Eastport for the night, as he had not been there in years. He said he really didn't need to get home until the 3rd. Retirement you know.

All in all, a great day in Maine.

That's how it is here. Thanks, Lois. Thanks, lady in the Hyundai. Happy 85th birthday to Phil of Mapleton, Maine.

I am far less jaded tonight and look forward to returning to Bangor P.D. in the morning. There are great people out there and sometimes you just have to stand on the side of the road to find them.

Maybe it was the timing of that story; maybe it was the poorly written simplicity about an old man traveling though Maine and meeting ladies with hammers and floor jacks. I look back and I really cannot put my finger on why that story worked on that particular day, but it did.

I learned that people were looking for things other than raves and rants, angry tirades, and memes. I found that people were looking for simple stories about everyday interactions between the co-habitants of this planet. I never worried again about the negative comments on being too wordy.

In essence, Phil Winslow and his flat tire freed me to just write.

I'll never be a world-class wordsmith, but I think my decades of just noticing the little things was presented to a large audience that day.

Maine is a special place—rural and raw, but also pleasant and personable. I decided to just tell the stories of Mainers and their interactions with our cops, and anyone else who showed up in the meantime.

It's worked out okay.

Acknowledgments

The journey to completing this project—like on all of our journeys—was peppered with people who helped along the way. My "significant other," who I write about quite regularly, was the first person who threw a MacBook in my lap to tell me I should write down some of the stories that have affected me. She prodded me along, left me alone, and said regularly, "You should go to camp this weekend and write. You always sound happy when you call me from the camp."

The fact of the matter is that I write best when I am left alone for a few days, and she recognized it. She's a special person to have put up with me for this long. Thanks, Amos. 143.

To my mom and dad, Art and Carol, thanks for loving me. Not everyone gets a good parent, let alone two. It should be noted that I wasn't always sleeping in the back pew when I put my head down. Sometimes, I was daydreaming, but I was still listening. Growing up with a minister as your dad guaranteed that you were always being watched by several angry little church ladies. This also meant that on many Sunday afternoons you were incarcerated in your bedroom for the dirty deeds you had done (dirt cheap) during Sunday school. The ladies would always rat me out. It was good for me. You both are good for me, and I thank you for understanding that it takes some time to mature. You have given me fifty-six years to practice. Thanks for telling me that you liked the things that I wrote. While I don't like to hear it, I still hear YOU. It means a lot.

I'd like to thank Bill Prest, my English teacher from high school. A war-injured Vietnam veteran with a masterful way of making you want to listen to him; Bill had an insightful way of throwing me out of class. As I meandered down the hall to the main office, I would look back and notice that he was smirking about whatever stupid thing I had just done. It wasn't a look of approval, just a look of understanding.

I can't say as I remember how to diagram a sentence, but I do recall his positivity when I did write something that looked even better after I recognized that the red pen marks were meant to make me better. Later in life, when I was working in radio, Bill and his wife Donna let me rent a room in their home. Being a twenty-year-old rock n' roll news guy/disc jockey didn't pay much, and they didn't charge me much. My room was by the backdoor, so I think was marginally better than having a dog to watch the place, and since I had my own bathroom, the yard was cleaner.

Bill stops by, or calls, about once a year, now. A couple of summers ago he pulled into the dooryard just to ask why I hadn't written the book yet. To have a teacher remember you forty-years after you walked out of his last class pretty much sums up how Bill Prest treats all the students that he taught; I am not special, but he made us all feel that way.

Thanks to all the cops who let me tell the stories on the Book of Faces, if it hadn't been for the Bangor Police Facebook page, no one would have seen a lot of the stuff I wrote. It allowed me to be creative in the presentation of cops, and I think adding a dash of humor and sarcasm has made it more palatable for the audience. It also forced me to move my other writing to my own page, and while I write more there, I still relish presenting the good things cops do to over three-hundred thousand people every day. Thanks to Chief Mark Hathaway for letting me do things that, for a time on Facebook, were uncommon. Many police departments have changed the way the write and present their pages, but I think we were early on the train. I believe, that overall, it's been positive for law enforcement.

Thanks to Melody Blake. While she is known as the Queen of the Front Desk at Bangor P.D., she spent her formative years as a proofreader for some big-time publishers. She has perused more than a few final drafts, and she found things that I would never have seen.

What are the chances that she would show up in the same time frame that I started writing regularly? It should also be noted that I was the polygraph examiner during Melody's hiring process before she took the job at our police department. This allowed me to pay her far less than her actual market value. I am kidding, of course. Blake made me a better writer, helped me calm down with the commas, and mitigated my under-utilization of M-dashes. She loves the work of E.B. White as much as I do and has cheered me on when I was slogging through long periods of writer's block. Part of her payment for her help is that I am using my tractor to remove some fallen spruce and poplar trees from her dooryard this coming spring. This is how we do "professional publishing" in Maine.

On the journey I spoke to, and met with, some great editors at some very well-known publishing houses. One in particular, who

I will not name for various reasons, called me after reading the page for a while. She was kind, considerate, and urged me to try to publish a book. I spoke to her on several occasions and while we did not get together on a project, her attention to what I was doing was evident and positive. That call, on a hot Friday in the summer of 2017, was truly a catalyst for the events from that point forward. I think it's important to thank the people who prod you along during a journey. Thanks C. J.

Doug Mayer, from Car Talk, thanks for reaching out to me to write for the website. Doug is a positive guy who read a couple of things that I wrote and felt I would be a good fit in a place where my stuff almost didn't fit. Yet he drove to Bangor from New Hampshire, via Cambridge, and bought me a pretty good cheeseburger. We talked, I wrote, and it put me in front of a different set of eyes. It was good for me, and there was no stress. Thanks, Doug.

Michael Steere, from Down East Books, sent me an email after I had decided that I was not going to publish a book. I was not downtrodden, or forlorn about it at all. I had been clear to some publishers that I wasn't really writing the things that they wanted. I have always said that anyone can write a book, I really would be more comfortable if a book that I wrote would sell a few copies. Not a lot, but at least enough so that some of them did not end up in a landfill in Asia (shout out to Doug Mayer for that analogy).

Michael Steere could be a psychologist; he just listens well. I told him that I had a fiction book I was writing, but that it wasn't done yet. Other than that, I wrote essays and short stories. I had been told by more than one person that a collection like that would never sell. I believed them, for they were the professionals.

Steere just said that he thought that we could sell that book. He didn't make promises of wealth and fame, just that he believed

I had an audience who would like to have a book like that. We talked about a timeline, shook hands, and talked from time to time about how the project would look. That's what I needed. I grew up in a place where a handshake is far more important than a contract. I knew I would live up to the deal, and I knew that Michael would, too. We later made it official. I think Michael probably had to sell the idea to some folks who wouldn't understand that he found me on Facebook, but it all worked out.

I hope you like the book; I do, but not everyone will. I believe the small stories are the important stories. For it is the people that we bump into, along the way, that really are sending us off on our way with a wink, or a slap on the back. The big stories happen, but they don't happen that often, and this book isn't one of them. There are no Feds, dragons, or explosions. There are only stories that I believe are worth telling. Thanks, Michael, for helping me do that.

Be well,
Tim Cotton